Triu  r

- Pain -

The No-Cost Solution

Covering

12 Medical Conditions including

Addiction and **Obesity**

Editor-In-Chief Harriet Clyde Kipps
Cover Art by Neil Edward Smith

www.watercure2.org

4949 Birney Ave., Moosic, PA 18507

Message from Bob Butts: Ill health is a symptom of a weak immune system caused by not giving the body the materials it needs to heal itself. It is not a drug or procedure deficiency. All the medical research and every cent in the world will never cure one health problem because it is 100% impossible to do so when only symptoms are addressed.

FIRST EDITION

Copyright © 2011 www.watercure2.org

ISBN-10: 1456581031
EAN-13: 9781456581039

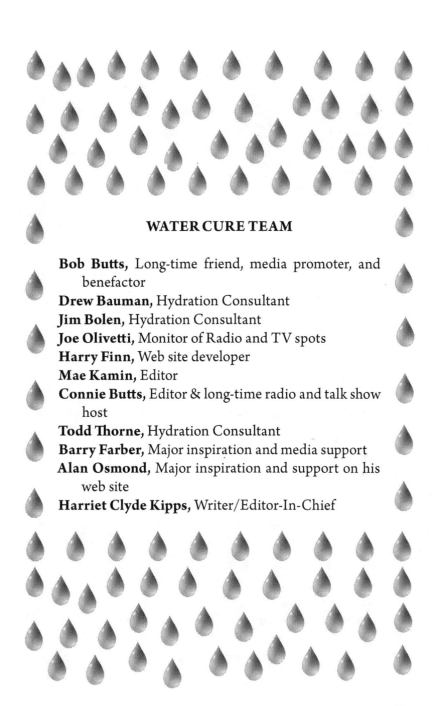

WATER CURE TEAM

Bob Butts, Long-time friend, media promoter, and benefactor

Drew Bauman, Hydration Consultant

Jim Bolen, Hydration Consultant

Joe Olivetti, Monitor of Radio and TV spots

Harry Finn, Web site developer

Mae Kamin, Editor

Connie Butts, Editor & long-time radio and talk show host

Todd Thorne, Hydration Consultant

Barry Farber, Major inspiration and media support

Alan Osmond, Major inspiration and support on his web site

Harriet Clyde Kipps, Writer/Editor-In-Chief

DISCLAIMER

The information and recommendations on water intake presented in this book are based on the research of F. Batmanghelidj, M.D., as found in his book, *"Your Body's Many Cries for Water."* The authors of this book, *"Triumph Over Pain,"* do not dispense medical advice or prescribe the use of the discontinuance of any medication as a form of treatment without the advice of an attending physician, either directly or indirectly.

The intent of the authors is only to offer information on the importance of water to well-being and to help inform the public of the damaging effects of chronic dehydration to the body - from childhood to old age

This book is not intended as a replacement for sound medical advice from a physician. On the contrary, sharing of the information contained in this book with the attending physician is highly desirable. Application of the information and recommendations described herein are undertaken at the individual's own risk. Very sick persons with past history of major diseases and under professional supervision, particularly those with severe renal disease, should not make use of the information contained herein without the supervision of their attending physician.

All the recommendations and procedures herein contained are made without guarantee on the part of the authors or the publisher, their agents, or employees. The authors and publisher disclaim all liability in connection with the use of information presented herein.

TABLE OF CONTENTS

[Many more *health problems are covered in the testimonials of* <u>*www.watercure2.org*</u>]

PROLOGUE

- 👍 **Dedication**
- 👍 **Preface**
- 👍 **Acknowledgments**

DEDICATION

This book is dedicated to the memory of
F. Batmanghelidj, M.D.

F. Batmanghelidj, M.D.

All that we have learned in order to help countless people is 100% because of what we have learned from the discoverer of the Water Cure, F. Batmanghelidj, M.D. Without him and his tireless research, his wonderful books would never have been written, and countless thousands of lives would never have been saved. In addition, not one single word in this book would ever have been written.

Every testimonial herein is a testimonial as to what Dr. Batmanghelidj has done for the benefit of all humanity. This book proves that nothing is impossible to the degree serving humanity is more important than serving ourselves.

While we often learn about evil and corrupt big pharmaceutical companies, I realize that it isn't true. The problem is that virtually every government, business and most of us are addicted to money, which has literally made it impossible for us to have a safe, healthy, happy and responsible world.

Dr. B. gave me the opportunity to help the man who made the greatest discovery in history. I worked with Dr. B. from August 1994 until the time of his death in November 2004 — the greatest experience of my life.

— Bob Butts

In Dr. B.'s own words...

"You are not sick, you are thirsty."

Message from Bob Butts: Dr. B.'s work is now available in 15 languages worldwide. Entire countries have adopted "The Water Cure" with gratifying results.

PREFACE

T*riumph Over Pain* is not only a reference for your information about these diseases, but an open invitation to satisfy your curiosity about a simple remedy for many illnesses — the Water Cure. Your questions will be answered with words you don't have to look up in a medical dictionary.

Sufferers from many diseases have success eliminating debilitating medications and turning to water for the cure. Examples include MS sufferer Alan Osmond of the Osmond family, who sought information for his MS from our Water Cure site and got some relief in hours from this so-called incurable disease, and continues to improve.

Also, National Baseball League All-Star catcher, Brian Mc-Cann, solved a chronic dry-eye problem, which threatened his career. By drinking water, he has rid himself of the glasses that bothered him during his games. Thanks to his eye doctor telling him to quit caffeine and drink water, his eye problem vanished, and in July 2009 he hit the game-winning hit that gave the National League their first ALL STAR win since 1996. For more information, Google *"Intravenous versus Oral Rehydration: Which is Best for Your Athlete?"*

In addition, Google "Poor Man's Gatorade," and learn why some entire nations call a similar method a "Magic Bullet." Their method is endorsed by the World Health Organization and UNICEF.

A prime example of an entire nation benefitting from a water-based cure is Bangladesh, which has used a cheap, trusted dehydration home remedy (a pinch of salt, a fistful of sugar, a half liter of water) for over 30 years. Over the past two decades, its overall child death rate has dropped threefold to five percent today.

> **Message from Bob Butts:** Google "Harvard Health Review, 40 million rescued with water, salt, and sugar."

At this time, the Water Cure is sweeping Russia, and doctors are recommending it to their patients. People say it is curing everything.

Finally, go to the website, watercure2.org, and view the television news specials, more testimonials, contact and other information.

ACKNOWLEDGMENTS

All of the people who deserve recognition on this page are too numerous to mention. They include the people who just "dropped in" at CeeKay Auto simply to thank us for having the web site, media coverage, etc., on the Water Cure, or who simply wished to comment on the loaner Water Cure books that they were returning so that others could learn from them. We thank all of them and wish them well with their health concerns as they apply the Water Cure to their pains and illnesses.

We would like to take personal note of the contributions of Mae Kamin, who worked diligently to edit, research and check for accuracy; Harry Finn, who worked tirelessly with our web site; Drew Bauman, who serves as a Hydration Coach helping people world-wide and whose health challenges he overcame under the personal guidance of Dr. Batmanghelidj; Joe Olivetti, who proofs all of our radio and TV spots, and connected us with Alan Osmond; and Jim Bolen, whose constant input to people worldwide is changing countless lives. (Jim's experience and insight is as close to Dr. B. as we could ever get. He knows Dr. B's work inside out.)

We would like to make a special tribute to Barry Farber and Alan Osmond, who have been major inspirations with their tremendous input and support, and a special thank you to Connie Butts for her dedication to this project (see page 9).

Those providing detailed testimonials of their successful experiences with the Water Cure are the backbone of this book, and they deserve accolades for their willingness to relive their former pain through their writing to share their experiences with others among our readers who are suffering from dehydration-related illnesses.

Message from Bob Butts: Harriet Clyde Kipps, working with the "Water Cure Team" (see p.iii), assumed the formidable task of garnering the massive amount of information and expressions of gratitude from around the world regarding Dr. B's work, and synthesizing it into this book, "Triumph Over Pain." She has designed the book's format to serve as an easy-to-use resource for individual sufferers of so-called "incurable" diseases, the research world, the education system (including the high-school level), focus groups, the health organizations, and the medical profession. Her dedication to this project is hereby acknowledged and greatly appreciated. *(For more about our Editor-in-Chief, See page 267.)*

Please Note a special tribute by Alan Osmond of the Osmond Family, a statement by noted talk-show host Barry Farber, and statements by other dedicated Water Cure supporters, in the Appendix.

Alan Osmond   Barry Farber

SPECIAL ACKNOWLEDGMENT

By Bob Butts

I want to express my gratitude to my "Water Cure Widow," my wife, Connie, who not only provided encouragement, motivation, and support, but who also took active part in making this book all that it can be. Connie did research, edited, proofread, and performed other tasks, often tedious ones, to help make this book a fine resource for those suffering from dehydration, the cause of most diseases, so that they, in turn, will help others to get well.

Also, I would like to thank Connie for her five years hosting our radio show, *Positive Press Radio*, where Dr. F. Batmanghelidj and Dr. Lorraine Day were regular guests. These interviews are archived on watercure2.org.

TRIBUTES

- 👍 **F. Batmanghelidj, M.D.**
- 👍 **Bob Butts**

THE INSPIRATION FOR THIS BOOK:

Fereydoon Batmanghelidj, M.D.

When Dr. Batmanghelidj thinks of a glass of water, he doesn't think of it as half full or half empty. He thinks of it as brimming over with the essentials of life. He thinks of it as the solvent of our lives and the deliverer of ripe old age. He thinks of it as the wave of the future. — The Washington Times

F. Batmanghelidj, M.D.

K nown everywhere as "Dr. B." or "Dr. Batman," Dr. Ferrydoon Batmanghelidj is an internationally-renowned researcher, author, and advocate of the natural healing power of water. He was born in Iran, but studied medicine in Scotland and England.

He returned to Iran and then became a political prisoner when the Iranian Revolution broke out. While in prison, he treated over 3,000 ill prisoners with water alone. On his release from prison, Dr. B. came to America in 1983, where he conducted research at the University of Pennsylvania on the effects of dehydration on the body from 1983 to 1989. He discovered that dehydration produces pain.

Dr. B. finished his first self-help book, *"Your Body's Many Cries for Water,"* in 1992. He devoted the last twenty years of his life promoting public awareness of the healing power of water, with several additional books following on specific diseases that are cured by water. These books include *Arthritis and Back Pain; ABC of Asthma, Allergies & Lupus; Water: Rx for a Healthier Pain-Free Life; Obesity, Cancer and Depression; You're Not Sick, You're Thirsty; Water: For Health, For Healing, For Life; Water Cures: Drugs Kill.*

This book, *"Triumph Over Pain,"* is a tribute to his work, providing testimonials "in their own words" by people who discovered and benefitted from the Water Cure. Dr. B. died in 2004 in Virginia.

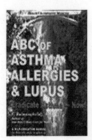  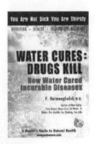

A PERSONAL GLIMPSE OF BOB BUTTS

{ In his own words }

"It would be a shame to die without winning at least one victory for humanity." *–Bob Butts*

I first heard the words above on a TV show in the 1950s called "Public Defender" starring E.G. Marshall. I said to myself, "That is what I want to make sure that I do." Ever since I met F. Batmanghelidj, M.D., discoverer of the Water Cure, and committed 75% of our ad budget to promote the Water Cure, I knew that was going to be part of my victory.

In 1937, my mother, Betty I. Butts, died of TB just before my second birthday, and in 1958 my best friend, my grandmother, Marion Cramer, died from cancer.

So why are all the groups who protested this unnecessary animal experimentation remaining silent now that many of these so-called incurable illnesses are being cured just by correcting the dehydration that caused them?

The Water Cure is it, and the best part is no one can make a dime on it, it has no side effects, *and it works*. I have seen people cured from many afflictions.

I am happy to announce that we will have a separate book on pets. I've always loved animals, especially dogs. Every dog I ever had was "the best of them all." It was a great thrill when I had the opportunity to work with two doctors and Pete, the dog, who had cancer. His tumor shrunk 50% in three days after sea salt was put in his food and water.

The full story is in the pet health testimonials section of our website — www.watercure2.org. I have heard of only one time where it allegedly failed to cure pet arthritis, hip displasia, or any back problem. The information proves that the cause of many pet health problems was salt deficiency, including arthritis where a 99% success rate was noted. My shock was when not one animal rights organization, or even the SPCA, the Humane Society, or the PETA had any interest in its discovery. All but one veterinarian had no interest, no matter how many pets got well.

Another big surprise was that, even though millions of little animals are put to death annually in research labs (allegedly to look for cures for diseases that the free Water Cure routinely cures), there wasn't any interest, and there still isn't any. While these little animals suffered and died, no one cared about preventing their needless pain and suffering. Was it because of all the money made on its research? And why are all the groups who protested this animal healing remaining silent?

GENERAL INTRODUCTION

GENERAL INTRODUCTION

This introduction is based on the work of F. Batmanghelidj, M.D.

Heartburn? Migraine Headaches? Anginal pain? Lower back pain? Morning sickness during pregnancy? Rheumatoid joint pain? Bulimia? Are these pains plaguing you? These pains are newly understood, drastic ways of showing dehydration. Your body will show its urgent need for water through these and other types of pain. Dehydration can hurt you irreversibly if not corrected. Your plum-like cells become prune-like.

Depending on the degree of dehydration, as well as the extent and the location of acid buildup inside the cells - when greater flow of water should have cleared the acid from that area - the classic pains of the body are produced. Pain is not always caused by injury or infection. It can be produced by dehydration, a simple mechanism of pain production that has eluded the medical field for time immemorial.

The drug industry spends billions of dollars researching pain-killers, and even more money advertising their particular brand of pain medication. I don't believe the answer is in these medications, however. Dehydration can be cured by water, for free.

To understand dehydration's main production in the body, we first need to learn about the way the acid-alkaline balance in the body works. Acid causes irritation of certain nerve endings. When the irritation occurs, the brain is alerted about the chemical environmental change which is felt as pain. In other words, it is the acidity in the body that causes pain.

Water washes the acidity out of the cell and makes the cell interior alkaline - the essential and normal state. For optimum health, the body should maintain an alkaline state -pH 7.4 is the desired level.

As an example, historic monuments and statues are damaged by pigeon droppings, which are highly acidic and eat into the stone. In time, the statues and monuments are unrecognizable as they lose their features. The DNA in the nucleus inside the cells of the body is alkaline and, like stone buildings, is also sensitive to the corrosive effects of acidity.

The kidneys play a role in removing acidity from the body through the urine that is formed, helping to keep the body's interior alkaline. Clear urine is an indicator of efficient acid-clearing. Dark yellow or orange urine is a sign of acid burns in the interior of the body. People who avoid drinking water to avoid urinating too much are ignorant of how they are hurting their bodies.

Although the brain gets priority for delivery of water for all its needs, the rest of the body is not so fortunate. With persistent dehydration, however, the brain also becomes damaged from acidity in the cells, with possible consequences such as Alzheimer's disease, Multiple Sclerosis, and Parkinson's disease.

It is documented that over 110 million people in America are experiencing pain because of dehydration. This figure is credited to Dr. B.'s research and is detailed in his book, *"Your Body's Many Cries for Water."*

Excerpted from *"Water for Health, for Healing, for Life,"* a masterpiece by F. Batmanghelidj, M.D.

> Also see: *"The importance of pH"* in the back matter of this book, an excerpt from Dr. Batmanghelidj's article on the subject.

PREVIEW OF TESTIMONIALS

PREVIEW OF TESTIMONIALS

> **Message from Bob Butts:** Michael Krol, one of our most spectacular testimonials; rid of handicapped license with two months.

AMPUTATION

ARTHRITIS
"I could not get out of bed for three months as the
chronic fatigue, loss of consciousness, and
pain associated with the fibromyalgia was
debilitating. After less than a week I decided
not to take my hormones and realized my hot
flashes were gone... completely gone! I started
sleeping through the night. My fibromyalgia
was gone, my chronic fatigue was gone, my
menopause symptoms were gone, my anxiety
and bouts of crying had disappeared too. I

BACK PAIN

CANCER

DEPRESSION

Depression story from Bob Butts: After being invited to speak at a counseling center dealing with long-term people so depressed they could not work, my one-hour talk was so successful that every patient was discharged within three weeks after using the Water Cure. I was never allowed back.

<u>DIABETES</u>

<u>EDEMA</u>

"Thank you for such a simple and inexpensive cure
for my problem. A radio saved my life. I was
working on a video project when I heard a

Message from Bob Butts: Dr. Batmanghelidj and I were the guests on the Art Bell Show mentioned above. Unfortunately, after a second appearance, we were not allowed on again. Most radio and TV shows NOW will not allow any Water Cure discussion to air no matter how many great testimonials are given. There is obviously no Interest in promoting a free solution to high profit health or any other problems.

<u>HEADACHES</u>

<u>HEART DISEASE</u>

"I am was so lucky to have a friend who provided me
    with the book that led me back to health. After
    being told I needed a heart transplant but was
    too far gone and wouldn't survive the surgery,
    the Water Cure fully restored my heart and

> **Message from Bob Butts:** Mayo Clinic tells how to prevent heart attacks with water. See WORDS FROM THE WISE section.

OBESITY

Message from Bob Butts: *Woman's World* detailed many Water Cure success stories under the title "The Slimming New Water Cure." It made the *Woman's World* front cover five times. Google the title and see for yourself.

R.S.D.: THE SUICIDE DISEASE

TESTIMONIALS

INTRODUCTION

This book is about the Water Cure and the people it restored to health - a life-saving solution primarily of sea salt and water, the foundation of life after no medical solution has been found. Entire countries have tried it as a last resort when money was not available for treatment from medical professionals. It has been called "the magic bullet." It has been a phenomenal success for these countries (see Appendix). Yet, having been introduced to America almost 30 years ago, the Water Cure has been mostly ignored because it works at no cost.

The target of this book is all debilitating pain, but R.S.D. (Reflex Sympathetic Dystrophy) is the worst pain known to man. R.S.D. is sometimes called the "Suicide Disease" because the pain from it is the worst known to man. People often kill themselves to escape it. It was first given that name during the Civil War. The pain gets so intense in the arms and legs of its victims that they sometimes choose to have their limbs amputated, only to have the pain come raging back into the stumps. (Can you imagine having this done to you?)

My first contact with R.S.D. was when an Old Forge nurse, Donna Riviello, called me wanting to know if the Water Cure could help her. Although stricken for many years, she had been bedridden for the last two years with the disease and knowing nothing about this problem, I asked Donna to describe the symptoms to me. Then I told her I knew the R.S.D. cause and cure, because it was obvious.

I told her that the symptoms she described were simply symptoms of dehydration, nothing mysterious or incurable. I told her that the Water Cure would quickly eliminate most of her symptoms, which it did. Within two weeks, only 25% of her pain remained after correcting her dehydration. All other symptoms were gone. In fact, her depression and suicidal tendencies were the first to go in a few days. Her complete testimonial is found in Chapter One.

"Theories" and "guesses" and "maybes" are terms used in treatments for R.S.D. now, with the most obvious one being overlooked. A hospital's own #1 protocol is a saline IV solution - salt and water! The Water Cure consists of sea salt and water, exercising daily - walking being the best, eliminating caffeine, alcohol and soda, while making some dietary adjustments, and adding a few supplements that together correct the pH, thereby strengthening the immune system so it can heal the body.

When it comes to the Water Cure curing countless people of alleged incurable diseases, not one researcher will even talk to us, even though our success rate is near 100% with some simple problems like asthma, allergies, chronic fatigue, depression, and arthritis to name a few. Then again, what financial incentive is there for anyone to endorse a solution to a high profit problem? Would you if your life depended on that income???? That's why medical science hasn't cured one major health or other high-profit problem since 1955 when it cured Polio. Dr. Dean Burk, founder of the National Cancer Institute told me back in the 1960's. "The more people making a living off cancer (that also applies to almost all high-profit problems), the more impossible it is to get rid of it."

In the ensuing pages, you will learn from testimonials of many individuals who found not only relief with the Water Cure, but often a complete cure. It is a life-saving solution in many areas where no medical solution has ever been found. General information on the history of the Water Cure, Water Cure Protocol, Water Cure consultants, answers to questions, etc., appear later in this book.

Yours in good health,
Bob Butts

CHAPTER ONE: R.S.D.

Introduction

R.S.D. has stumped the professionals. The treatments by doctors are described as "theories" when asked about curing this painful disease. Also, although the medication used by doctors to treat R.S.D. admittedly is not approved by the FDA, they feel that it "might" be beneficial and is "worth a try." Such vague responses only serve to cause additional concern for the patient, and the medication has not demonstrated any significant relief.

Even though it is estimated that up to 750,000 people have the disease, including celebrity Paula Abdul, which keeps it in the headlines, it has been without a pain-eliminating solution... *until now*. Sadly, science has no interest, no matter how many people get well. It is vital, if we want any integrity in medicine, that all campaign contributions from drug companies to legislators be ceased.

R.S.D. is known by a half dozen names, including: Reflex Sympathetic Dystrophy Syndrome (R.S.D.), Shoulder-Hand Syndrome, and Sudeck's Atrophy. Yet, there is one name for the disease that is used more frequently by people who are familiar with it - "The Suicide Disease."

Such a high number of triggers is not true of other medical conditions and only adds to the vague nature of information coming from the medical field on R.S.D. Most experts' suggestions for R.S.D. relief are "guesses" - tagged with the statement "Not confirmed by clinical studies." The vagueness continues. But it should be obvious to science that according to F. Batmanghelidj, M.D. all pain is the result of acid burn from low alkalinity-high acid conditions.

Now, let's talk about money. The cost of these apparent blunders is phenomenal, thus overloading an already financially-bloated medical profession. These high costs affect all of us. Are they necessary? "The best things in life are free!" That statement has been around a long time. One of the most significant "freebies" that we get in life is "our brain." As relief for R.S.D. patients through the medical profession becomes less and less of a reality, it is time to use the free gift and question... question... question.

The following question is for all those concerned with R.S.D. - personally, in the family, among close friends - to consider:

Message from Bob Butts: What if the cure were proven and free?

That's right! Available at no cost to the patient through a proven method. **How can this be?** There is a simple explanation.

Message from Bob Butts: R.S.D. is nothing more than severe dehydration.

In other words, "The patient is not sick, he is thirsty!" Understandably, proof is appropriate at this point, and it is available in this book. How? Through testimonials from R.S.D. patients who have tried a simple treatment based on water - and were greatly improved. So far, people are getting rid of most symptoms and 75 to 80 percent of their R.S.D. pain, along with most of the rest. The common denominator we have found on each of the victims was dehydration. Victims must realize that caffeine, alcohol and soda are diuretic drinks which can disable their immune systems, which causes the pain, as does insufficient water and sea salt. And they must consider diet and salt balance.

Testimonials: The following testimonials are from victims of R.S.D. who have found the "Water cure." The research of F. Batmanghelidj, M.D. on pain confirms all of this.

Todd Thorne, Pittston, PA

There are people who believe that things in life happen for a reason. Sometimes what happens - no matter if it is a good thing, or a bad thing, a funny thing or very serious - it makes you who you are and teaches the person a lesson in life and self-understanding. Even if the happening is traumatic or enlightening, it will eventually make that person grow emotionally and spiritually. I am one of those people who believe that it can and will bring new meaning to self-enlightenment.

More than seven years ago, I was beginning a new phase in my life that was supposed to bring about positive changes, not only for myself, but for my entire family. I was a nurse/paramedic who wanted more out of life than my current education provided me. So, I went back to college in pursuit of a Physician's Assistant (P.A.) degree. I handled the first two years of college rather well, getting above average GPAs. But, in doing this college thing, I knew that I still had to work to bring in money to support my family. So I took a side job that was offered to me by an old high school friend who was the plant manager of a facility. Upon visiting the plant and sitting down with that old friend, I made him aware that I had undergone a few injuries along my way in life. He hired me anyway.

Three months into working, I literally got the shock of my life. The shock was from a malfunctioning machine that jolted me with 480 volts of electricity at 60 amps of current. It wasn't until nine hours after the accident that I woke up in a hospital bed looking at my wife and two boys. No one knew what actually happened.

During the next 18 months, I was bounced back and forth between cardiology and neurology with each medical field saying that my problems lay with the other. Finally, as a new doctor at the hospital was brought into my case, I got a definitive answer to my problems. The doctor is an "Electro-Physiologist." He diagnosed with a Chronic Pain disease called R.S.D. (Reflex Sympathetic Dystrophy). But, even with that diagnosis, I was still having other problems and was referred to yet another doctor in another field called Endocrinology.

Come to find out that, when the electricity entered my body, it traveled up through my autonomic nervous system up to my brain stem to where two major parts of the brain lie - the Thalamus and the Hypothalemus. These two parts are what control all of my involuntary organs, including my heart.

The electricity affected them in a way that they were now only working at about 15% capacity.

I was now diagnosed with P.A.D. (Pure Autonomic Dysfunction). So, along with having the R.S.D. and this Autonomic Dysfunction, I was put on a regimen of medications that numbered up to 14 pills a day - ranging from pills to stabilize my organ hormones to controlled substance pain medications.

But all this time I was still battling the effects of the electricity on my body, as it was deteriorating my body to an unusable stage.

Now that I was completely out of work, I was trying to get our car back in working condition as I couldn't afford to take it to a garage. But I guess it was a little too much strain on my body, as diseases took over and sped up the deterioration and knocked me so far down that I was now confined to a wheelchair. Some days the pain gets to me to the point I just ask God to take me already. Then I look at my wife, my kids, my dog and cat, and I realize that these people and pets need me.

When one of my friends, Denise DeBiasi, from CeeKay Auto Stores' Pittston store saw me in that condition as I wheeled by her, she told me about Mr. Bob Butts and the Water Cure that has helped other people like me with R.S.D. I took home the papers and the CD that she gave me. I listened to the CD and read the papers intently.

I knew I had to try something, anything, because what all these pain doctors did was fill me with pills that basically were turning me into a wasted zombie. I could not let myself, at the age of 43, give up and just waste away.

It took a little while for my body to adjust because of the different things I had to give up, and introduce a new way of living. But I was still fighting the effects of the electricity on my body. So my case was a lot different than what Mr. Butts would normally see. In my opinion, it usually should only take maybe up to two weeks to improve a person, but with me it took almost the next two years.

When I started the Water Cure I saw something happening that amazed me. With the feeling starting to return to my legs, I saw the now dormant nerves start waking up and actually jumping at least ½ inch through my skin. The doctors thought it was their doing because I was starting to get better, but it wasn't. I told them that I started the Water Cure and those doctors who plied me with all those meds told me to never return to their offices. They did not want to help me anymore if I continued to use a "fake" treatment. Hundreds of thousands of dollars were spent on orthodox medicine, while only a few dollars for food and supplements are spent with the Water Cure.

> **Message from Bob Butts:** I think that anyone who gets better after using a free solution should get a 200% refund for all the money wasted that failed. Then there would be a lot more incentive to do what is right Instead of what's profitable. Doctors should also get a refund because they were not taught recognize the obvious cause of R.S.D. Almost every symptom was obviously the result of dehydration, which I recognized immediately when I asked people to describe their symptoms.

Even the physical therapy I was getting was discontinued, partially from my using the Water Cure. But I saw more improvements in my body using the Water Cure than I saw with conventional medicine.

What I studied for many, many years for medical degrees failed me, and something that is virtually free did more for me and got me walking and driving a car again. I know I will never be able to return to my former employment in the medical field, but using the Water Cure has opened other avenues of life to me.

In conclusion, if it weren't for my friend telling me about Dr. Batmanghelidj's formula for the Water Cure, and Mr. Butts for having such a program out in the world, I know I wouldn't be able to do anything that I do today. I thank God for the Water Cure as it has actually saved my life.

R.S.D. is known as the "suicide disease" because, when a person has it, the disease causes so much pain that a person either dies from the pain stressing their hearts out or the person just can't handle it anymore and commits suicide.

I'm too young to die from a failed heart, and I'm still not so far gone that I would commit suicide.

Todd Thorne, Pittston, PA (update)

There are people out in the world with the same disease as I have and I found a way to be mostly out of pain. I tell myself that I can possibly help them the same way I was helped. It worked for me, so it could possibly work for other people. I found a purpose in life again, other than just sitting on my couch or staying in a wheelchair and grabbed it.

I had the determination to fight for my life. I got on something that 99% of the doctors refused to recognize as a viable method to help get rid of pain. But I used it and my own therapies to walk again. I refused to give up to the pain and fought it. I was on 14 medications per day because of it. I am now down to two different medications per day. I am basically about 80% out of pain. Not bad for having full body R.S.D. from being zapped by 480 volts on a 60 amp unit.

My health insurance provider spent over $300,000 to try to get me well. But for less than $10 the Water Cure got me out of the chair and I got rid of 80% of my pain.

Whether or not you have the support of ALL family members or friends, it's up to you to live, not them. One of my sisters told me that she didn't even want me to tell her anything about the disease from my injuries. She wanted to remember me the way I was before the accident. It's good to have a strong support team right by your side, but it's up to you to have the courage to get through every day. As long as you can look at yourself in the mirror, smile and say, "I am alive and I am going to take my life back," you can accomplish what you want. No, the pain is not all in your head. It's really there, but fight it, find other methods to fight it. Question everything the doctors want to do. Do research to find alternative methods out there to rid yourself of pain. *And then live again.*

> **Message from Bob Butts:** Over three hundred thousand dollars were spent on failed orthodox protocols to treat symptoms of Todd's R.S.D., and only a few dollars for food and supplements with the Water Cure got him out of his wheelchair. The same thing has happened many times with other health problems.

Donna Riviello, Old Forge, PA
I don't know where to begin. Maybe by stating what many people say: "Thank God you are alive."

But when you are suffering with intolerable pain and depression, we don't thank God. We question God. We pray to God and sometimes we even lose faith in God. But God watches and waits. It is in his time, not ours.

There is a difference between living and being painfully alive... only existing. Unfortunately, for 20+ years, I was painfully alive... only existing. I am a 53-year-old LPN who was diagnosed with the horrific chronic pain of Reflex Sympathetic Dystrophy (R.S.D.) in 1990. It took three years and over 15 doctors to get the diagnosis.

Message from Bob Butts: Considering all symptoms were obvious signs of dehydration, it should have been obvious to any M.D. provided he or she understands dehydration. (Dr. B. would have known them immediately. I - an auto parts business owner with proper training - knew them immediately. Of course, anyone trained by Dr. B. would also have known.)

These doctors all said I had many "syndromes" and named illnesses, such as :Fibromyalgia, neuralgia, shoulder/hand syndrome, CFS, Carpal Tunnel, and many more. I was a *walking syndrome, etiology unknown.* So, treatment/help was also unknown... non–existent... as I felt I was. The R.S.D. pain was in my left shoulder from a seatbelt injury, the result of a car accident. At the time I was working as a nurse, going to college at night, caring for my sickly parents, being a wife and a mother to my 15-year-old daughter and my five-year-old son. I had an active, busy life.

R.S.D. is the type of disease that will spread to any other injured body part, overuse of a limb, or just for no reason. This is what I was told by the doctors.

We are the only patients who BEG to have a limb amputated to rid us of the pain, or else - due to no cure or help - we commit suicide. R.S.D. is called the "suicide disease." (I know... I had my suicide all planned out.) It was then that I had to quit my job and rearrange every aspect of my life.

There are three stages of R.S.D. I was in stage one. I was told I could not work, could not lift anything over five pounds, could not lift my left arm above my head (doctors and therapists taught me how to take off a shirt without lifting my arm; NO more children... and to have a tubal ligation (not with general anesthesia because the placement of the breathing tube would spread it to my neck).

I had it under Versed, the first time ever used by my OB-GYN. NO novacaine because the needles will spread the R.S.D. to that area. No elective/cosmetic surgery, no unnecessary blood work, no tattoos or piercings, NO ANYTHING!

I was living in FEAR all those years, cloaked with the blanket of DOOM and GLOOM... diagnosis, R.S.D.! My poor son would fall and I would run to help him up, but could not pick him up... afraid I would get worse... go to stage two, or three (bedridden).

I was told I had to have AGGRESSIVE treatments: over 60 stellate angion nerve blocks (In 1990 they cost my insurance $3,000 EACH), spinal morphine pumps, HUNDREDS of trigger point injections... all with needles, but no novacaine - hypocrisy!

In 2000 I was threatened by a new doctor. He kept giving me the trigger point injections in my left shoulder, and they DID NOT HELP. Instead, they made me worse. He gave me eleven in one visit. It took him 30 seconds... cost, $300 EACH. And he REUSED needles. I had to ask him to change them in front of me!

The doses of meds were incredible. We R.S.D. people are Opiate resistant. I am in the five-foot range about 110 pounds. The meds I was on would kill a horse. Yet, I got NO RELIEF. This doctor said, if I did not take trigger point injections to my lumbar area (NEVER had pain in my legs) when it came time for my disability review, he would TELL THEM that I was refusing treatment that might help and get my disability stopped! So I got the injections, and the R.S.D. spread to my legs. This pain was 1,000 times worse than my shoulder.

So I stopped doing almost everything. No going to dinner, no movies, no parties, no shopping. I was not in a mall for 10 YEARS!

Twelve days of hospital errors/abuse in 2005 left me bedridden. I went to the ER with severe upper right abdominal pain at 9:00 a.m. A cat scan was done at 11:00 a.m. - diagnosis appendicitis... need emergency surgery. But it was Saturday, and the surgeon on call was GOLFING and REFUSED to come in. The hospital COULD NOT FIND another surgeon for eight hours, while I was in pain from appendicitis, according to the doctors!

By the time I had the surgery, my appendix was ruptured and gangrenous! I suffered many unnecessary life-threatening complications - peritonitis, blood poisoning, collapsed lungs, pleural effusions, phlebitis, and a slip and fall on spilled IV antibiotic that the nurse did not wipe up! Yet, I was refused a medical malpractice case because I had a pre-existing disability!?

I felt like a prisoner trapped in my own body/mind. My body was riddled with intolerable pain and my mind crippled with depression and DARK suicidal thoughts. I prayed to God daily for His mercy.

Due to all the trauma and unnecessary life-threatening complications, my R.S.D. spread throughout my body and was in a major flare-up. I was in bed 20-22 hours a day for the next two years. I also developed numerous other health problems such as constipation and rectal bleeding, weight gain and muscle atrophy of my left leg. Most were caused by medication, inactivity, dehydration and a poor diet (nutritional deficiencies). I was out of the house three times, total. My body was riddled with intolerable pain and my mind was crippled with depression, guilt, and even dark thoughts of suicide. I was "painfully alive," not living. Through my 20 years of horrific R.S.D. pain, I have had over 55 Stellate Ganglion Nerve Blocks, nine rib cage nerve blocks, Intra-Spinal Epidural Catheters, hundreds of trigger point injections, PI, Ot, acupuncture, other therapies, and have run the gamut with medications - all with minimal or no relief of pain. I felt helpless and hopeless.

On May 19, 2007, out of desperation, I saw a familiar ad in my local newspaper for the Water Cure. I had heard about it and knew people who had received benefit from it, but me? MISS R.S.D.? Oxycontin, Morphine, all types of needles and therapy did not help, so I NEVER gave the Water Cure a second thought... until now.

I called Bob Butts, who owns an auto parts store three minutes away from my home. He has been promoting the Water Cure in my area for 14 years, and it cost him over $600,000 of his own money... just to help others.

Now, thanks to the Water Cure, *I am happy to go to the grocery store, cook and clean like I used to do.*

I started Dr. Batmanghelidj's Water Cure. Within two weeks my pain had decreased 75%! My depression is gone, and I lost 28 unwanted pounds in five months! I NEVER had 75% relief of pain with any costly medication or painful treatment. All of the other health problems are also relieved or gone! I have now regained much of my life back simply by adding the proper amounts of sea salt and water to a more nutritious diet. I have stopped drinking any caffeine, coffee, soda or alcohol, which dehydrates our bodies. Dehydration is the cause of most disease, pain and illness.

Please check out my channel 22 News story, interview on FOX TV and WILK talk radio show at watercure2.org. Read the many testimonials of people helped or even CURED of diabetes, cancer, pain and many diseases. *Twenty years of pain 75 gone in two weeks!*

God has truly BLESSED me and shown me His mercy. He has given me a second chance... a new less painful life! Yet, the most amazing thing is that my 17 years of extreme pain, suffering and tears has enabled me the spiritual joy of helping others get well, too. Naturally, I don't want anyone to suffer needlessly the way I did.

Please help me help others obtain pain relief through the many miracles of the Water Cure. You can contact me at - bonita45@hotmail.com or Donna Riviello, Old Forge, PA 18518. Peace and healing.

John M., Avoca, PA

In 1989 I started having lots of pain in my legs. At the time I was an auto mechanic and my boss noticed that I was getting dizzy and staggering at work. I was forced to quit my job.

I went to my regular doctor, who sent me to the best neurosurgeon at Wilkes Barre General Hospital. The doctor sent me for X-rays that showed nothing. I then went for an MRI, and it showed that my spinal cord was choked, and the doctor suggested surgery.

The surgery replaced three discs and shaved another one open. Looking at the MRI after surgery showed that the spinal cord went back in place after the discs were replaced. The doctor stated that I should be 70% better in one year. However, I was 70% worse! I was in such bad shape that I qualified for a jazzy wheelchair.

In December 1990 I had another MRI. This time it showed that my spinal cord was in place and was healing. I told the doctor I now had massive pain in my hips, knees and ankles, so I had another MRI of those areas. This one showed massive arthritis in all three areas.

The doctor said there was nothing he could do except put me on pain pills. I went on morphine, oxycortin and others without any success in eliminating the pain. I even tried a series of synvich shots, which didn't help at all. In 1991 I went on vitamins/minerals and other supplements for 4-5 years with no noticeable difference.

I tried therapy for six months and was in more pain than without it. I tolerated the pain for many years. The pain was so severe that at times I considered committing suicide.

From 1989 to about 2008 I used the wheelchair and two canes. At this time I talked with Bob Butts from CeeKay Auto and he gave me literature and CDs on the Water Cure program. I thought he was nuts when he told me about the program.

This time I listened and started immediately on the Water Cure. Within about one-and-a-half months I began to notice improvement in pain relief.

Today I am walking without the two canes and have no use for the wheelchair. On a scale of one to ten, my pain was a ten and now is about a three. I have stopped going to doctors and I have stopped taking all pills completely.

Darrell Stoddard darrellstoddard@gmail.com
I couldn't walk across the floor for a hundred dollars a step when I first got up in the morning. My left ankle that I injured hurt so bad that I would nearly pass out if I put weight on it. Then, after hopping around on one foot for a while, I was able to hobble through the day. The thing that made my injury even more distressing is that I am a Pain Specialist who had stopped the pain in more than 9,000 patients, and I couldn't help myself.

My regular morning runs that I had been doing faithfully for 26 years came to an end. The goal of running like my acquaintance, Larry Lewis (who is 103 years of age and runs six miles every morning before going to work) was now impossible.

I had my foot X-rayed. There were no fractures or broken bones. I tried my own treatments - Bioelectric and Auricular Therapy. It did nothing for the pain. I had orthotics made, had my ankle taped, did all the exercises given to me by a podiatrist, injected my foot with Vitamin B-6 and B-12, injected all of the trigger points with procaine. I took vitamins and minerals of all kinds, tried gucosamine hydrochoride, phenylalsaine, blue-green algae, cod-liver oil, flaxseed oil and non-fat yogurt, pygnogiani, etc.

When all of the natural stuff failed, I tried aspirin, Tylenol, and a number of non-steroidal anti-inflammatory drugs. Some of these made the pain a little more bearable, but when I stopped taking them, the pain came back with a vengeance. I was obviously just masking the pain and making myself vulnerable for further injury. For nine months I tried everything ever heard of for pain, short of narcotics. By now I was getting desperate. My goal and dream of running until I was 100 years old was now just that - only a dream.

I read the book, *"Your Body's Many Cries for Water,"* by Dr. F. Batmanghelidj, that I highly recommend, and visited watercure2.org for further information. I started to drink more water, or at least thought I was, but I wasn't consistent enough to help, and my pain continued.

I started to consistently drink more water. Lo and behold, the painful foot that stopped me from running and crippled me for nine months got better.

Now each morning I can again go running like I did before the injury. Through the experience, I learned as much about stopping pain as I did in a lifetime of study. Dr Batmanghelidj is right. When we are in pain, our body "is crying for water."

Besides having the pain in my foot go away, another interesting change came into my life. Several times a day I have to run for the bathroom like a little child, something I hadn't done for more than 50 years. One of these days I'm not going to make it, but it will be worth it.

R.S.D.: A Final Word

I talked to many people with R.S.D. with no idea how many listened. But I never knew of one who wasn't dehydrated. I also don't know of one who did not get helped.

The truth is that R.S.D. is nothing but a fancy scary term for dehydration. Correct the dehydration and it starts to get better. It is insane to invent thousands of different disguises and names for the same villain.

Everyone, including all high school children and the elderly, should read Dr. B.'s books so they understand how and why they have their profitable illnesses.

The truth is that we are a nation so addicted to money, I can't think of one high-profit problem we can't solve, whether it is crime, health, mental health, or even wars.

The Water Cure is truly light years ahead of the entire world because it out-cares most of the rest of the world.

–Bob Butts

> **Peter Gott, M.D.'s Column on R.S.D., Scranton Times/Citizens Voice, 7/19/11:** *Writer who suffered from R.S.D. states:* "The best therapy is water therapy, which I still do." *The doctor's response:* "Hydrotherapy has been found to have been beneficial in the e-mails that I have received." *Medical report:* "Hydrotherapy is synonymous with the term Water Cure." *Dr. Gott is a retired General Internist.* (Bob Butts was interviewed by the Scranton Times in relation to this column. See watercure2.org.)

CHAPTER TWO: ARTHRITIS

Introduction

It is said Arthritis is a group of conditions involving damage to the joints of the body but that is not true. It is nothing more than the effect of extreme dehydration. When the dehydration is corrected, healing takes place.

There are over 100 different forms of arthritis, but only one cause. They are all the same thing - each with a different mask. Elderly people start to lose thirst perception, which makes all problems worse. Other arthritis masks are rheumatoid arthritis, psoriatic arthritis, and autoimmune diseases. This root cause is the same thing: chronic dehydration.

The major complaint by individuals who have arthritis is pain. Pain is often a constant and daily feature of the disease. The pain may be localized in the back, neck, hip, knee or feet. The pain from arthritis is due to acid burns because the pH is highly acidic. It is not a disease.

Testimonials: The following testimonials are from victims of arthritis (dehydration) who have found the Water Cure.

Robert Fairbain

It is totally amazing what the Water Cure has done for me. I just want to pass my thanks on for making this available to people. I was in pain 24/7 from arthritis and various injuries I have had over the years. I am cutting back on my narcotics with the hope that after a while I won't need them any more and I have already cut out the medicine I was taking for arthritis and my stomach.

It is such a relief that I may not need a lot of the stuff. I want to tell everyone about it. I have already got the rest of my family on it and a lot of my friends. They know the kinds of pain I have been in for years and years. I wish I had the money to spend the time to spread this around. I will do whatever I can though.

I want to thank you all for what you are doing and I hope you can continue to spread the word. Thank you for the biggest relief I have ever had.

Karen DeStefano, DeStefano@comcast.net

I was searching the Internet for information on Rheumatoid Arthritis and Lupus when I came across the Water Cure. My father had been suffering with various symptoms and was diagnosed with both of the above diseases, cycling between them at different times during the year. Having my own health issues, I was intrigued with what I was reading and decided logically that the Water Cure was not only the best answer for my father, but for myself as well.

I was suffering from intense menopausal symptoms: hot flashes every five minutes, sleeplessness, anxiety, crying, depression, fatigue. I was diagnosed with fibromyalgia, chronic fatigue and menopause.

My body ached and was swollen and stiff. At one point I was passing out if I exerted myself at all. I could not get out of bed for three months as the chronic fatigue, loss of consciousness and pain associated with fibromyalgia was debilitating. I would have one or two good days out of a month that I could function on my feet, but then it was back to bed as my energy would again become depleted.

At one point, I had resigned myself to the fact that this would be how my life would end and the best I could do was to try to be happy with what life dealt me and try to deal. I tried every day. I began going to a wellness center and was given a mass of supplements and put on hormone replacement therapy, which I began taking on a regular basis. This did help and I was happy to be going in the right direction. What I didn't realize then, though, was that it wasn't the supplements, but the water that I was drinking to take them that was bringing me back to health.

It was about a year and a half into my illness before I found the Water Cure online. It made perfect sense to me and I began to drink... and drink... and drink... and drink. Being afraid of the salt portion of the cure, I sort of avoided it at first, but then realized that I would be doing myself more harm than good if I didn't follow the recipe. I began adding salt, sea salt.

After less than a week I decided not to take my hormones one morning and realized that my hot flashes were gone... completely gone!

I started sleeping through the night. My fibromyalgia was gone, my chronic fatigue was gone, my menopause symptoms were gone, my anxiety and bouts of crying had disappeared, too. Every day I just get better and better. It is now about three weeks into the Water Cure story and I could not be happier.

Sadly, I cannot get my father to understand that his severe symptoms are the result of chronic and now critical dehydration. He is drinking some water to appease me, but still drinks his tea. He is 79 and just refuses to accept that free water, as opposed to expensive and debilitating medications, could be the answer. I am still committed to getting him to understand but, for some people, you just have to let them make their own decisions. I have resigned myself to accepting that my father, being on the path that he is, will not be with me much longer unless he changes his mind set and embraces water... the answer to recovery and life.

I praise Dr. Batman every day for bringing this simplistic miracle into my life, and for Bob Butts, who so unselfishly works to bring this miracle to others through his time, dedication and knowledge.

Jim Austin, Mountaintop, PA

In 1966 I was diagnosed with an Avascular Necrosis of the left hip. The doctor recommended bone graft surgery, with the procedure lasting 16 to 20 years. Four years later I fell at work, hurt the hip and, as a result, the hip had to be replaced. Two years later I was struck by a machine at work, which resulted in a back injury, also loosening the hip replacement. I had the hip replaced for a second time, but was told nothing could be done for the back pain. I had numerous epidural and facet blocks, but to no avail. I was put on anti-inflammatories and pain killers. For years I couldn't walk without a cane.

After seeing a commercial on TV about a year and a half ago, I decided to try the Water Cure. After about three months

I was able to stop using my cane, and after six months I stopped taking all of my medications. I walk much better now and live a life nearly pain-free.

The Water Cure is as simple as drawing water. Add a little sea salt that is available at any good health food store to the water and drink. It's the best thing I ever did for myself and I will continue to do it for the rest of my life.

> **Message from Bob Butts:** His German Shepherd was also cured of arthritis. See story on pet health page at www.watercure2.org

Mike Audet, Sr. mlaudet@msn.com

I am writing you a long overdue letter. I used to suffer from psoriatric arthritis in my hands and knuckle joints. My fingers were so swollen they looked like sausages. My knuckles were swollen, red, painful and hot to the touch. If I clenched my fists very tightly, my hands would bleed in many places through painful cracks. I had to wear white cotton gloves in order to avoid getting blood on everything I touched. I went to many doctors and dermatologists. No one had an answer and one even said it was the worst case of psoriatric arthritis he had seen. Did I say it was painful? So much so the pain would wake me up at night.

Then I read your article about sea salt about two years ago. I bought Redmond Sea Salt - the one mined in Utah. In just fifteen days after using it daily, the symptoms began to recede. Within a month I was as good as new. To this day, I have not had a recurrence. My friend who is my age had similar symptoms, but not as severe, was amazed and somewhat skeptical when I told him about the sea salt. He tried it and he has had no recurrence in a couple of years.

Thank you from the bottom of my heart.

P.S. I subscribe to your letter and enjoy it very much.

John Guy, sgt3884@yahoo.com

Water and salt have helped relieve my pain caused by ankylosing spondylitis, a form of arthritis. This is a hereditary condition with which my grandfather and mother were also afflicted. It was confirmed by my chiropractor after X-ray. The symptoms are hardening of the spine with resulting stooped position, difficulty turning the head from side to side, and iritis (inflamation of the iris).

I have read all of Dr. Batman's books, explored all of watercure.com and watercure2.org and listened to and watched all posted listings in the audio/video area. I follow the eight glasses daily with sea salt program as well as take vitamins, msm, omega-3 and glucosamine chondroltin. Since I began the eight glasses with salt daily regime, I have had less pain when walking up and down stairs, stand straighter, and have not had a recurrence of iritis. Since I have been drinking eight glasses of water with sea salt, I have experienced the aforementioned positive results.

I have shared my experience and told other people about what Dr. Batman has written in his books - most of them agree that drinking water is better, but I really can't say that I know of anyone who has tried the program other than myself. I have a friend who has severe migraine headaches. I showed her the area of Dr. Batman's book that deals with migraines, after which she informed me that it couldn't be true since her doctor would have told her if it was. She still has migraines.

Thank you, Bob, for your diligence in promoting Dr. Batman's message.

Christie Interlante, cilink@gte.net

I have been suffering with rheumatoid arthritis pain. The pain in my joints was so severe, I could hardly walk. I had spent so much time, energy and now most of the money I had saved, and still I was in pain. I had read about *The Body's Many Cries for Water* some time ago and I remembered it was very good, but only until recently, when a friend suggested that I read your book on RA and back pain, did I remember how potent the Water Cure could be. I started I started having most of the joint problems after I moved to the high desert. I didn't drink much water before I moved, and in the last two years I have not increased my intake of water.

After I read the book, I started drinking water in the AM, two glasses a half hour before a meal, then more water two hours after. I find I have usually had problems drinking water, but now, the more I drink, the more I want, and I am recognizing my so-called hunger as thirst.

For the first time in two years, I am once again able to walk over a mile at a time. I am experiencing less and less pain and swelling in my ankles, knees, wrists, and other joints. I am 30 pounds overweight, and hope that being able to walk and move will help this situation as well. Thank you.

Stephen B., stephenb2001@yahoo.com

After hearing you and Dr. B. on the Art Bell Show with Barbara Simpson, I tried the Water Cure. Having RA for the past

15 years, living with the disfigured/damaged joints for the past 10 years, I thought I was destined to be afflicted with this "disease" for life.

Over the past few months, my level of pain dramatically increased to the point of wanting to seek managed pain medications. Once on these medications, I knew my life would be altered dramatically, with severe stomach and liver problems arising from their use. I was suicidal! Chronic severe pain daily - pick a joint, any joint. I was days from seeking a doctor to give me those life-altering drugs.

Then I heard you and Dr. B. Try it, I thought, and I did. Please accept my great gratitude an appreciation for the relief this simple process has brought to my new life! Within four days the pain has subsided to the point where I cried from relief instead of crying from the pain. Thank you! Thank you, Dr. B.! My life is so altered for the better, and I see the best to come.

P.S. Now that my "vision" is clear - I see now that this increase in joint pain may have been a result of drinking a glass of wine daily, which I started 3-4 months back.... which I have STOPPED.

Mike George, Avoca, PA

About eight months ago, I had a talk with Bob Butts, owner of Cee-Kay Auto in Moosic, Pennsylvania. When Bob discussed "The Water Cure" with me, I laughed. I really laughed. But, I had this leg problem. My legs used to swell up really bad. I could hardly walk because of my arthritis and gout. I went to the doctor. He gave me anti-inflammatory pills. They just ended up ripping the gut out, so I stopped taking them.

Then when Bob talked to me again about your program, I decided to start it. I have kept it going for the last four to six months. Now I feel like a young person. I am 54 but I feel 20. I was ready to sell my business of 35 years and get rid of it. I figured that my legs were worn out. At least, that's what the doctors had told me. I needed joint, ankle, and knee replacements. I had one right knee done, but the left one I never went back for. The first one didn't do any good. My attitude changed greatly after I started drinking water.

When you're living in constant pain, your mind is only on one thing. I was just going to get rid of the business and say I can't do what I used to. I usually work 10 to 15 hours a day. I felt I might as well get out of the business.

Then I started just drinking water and adding a little salt on my food. My health has really improved in the last four to six months. I am not saying that is all because of the water. Maybe it is, maybe it isn't. All I know is that, since I have been following "The Water Cure" I have made "The Water Cure" a habit. I really feel much better and my wife will also tell you that I used to be nasty and very unpleasant to live with. Now all that has changed.

I have no problem with people contacting me about my health. When I talk to people about this, they laugh at me. Well, I laughed at it in the beginning, too.

Why water? Water has been around since the beginning of time. Instead of drinking coffee in the morning or milk like I used to, I go home for breakfast and I have a 12-ounce glass of water. I don't drink coke or beer with my meals, or anything else except for a 12-ounce glass of water. If I want a beer later, then I'll have one.

I can't say that my complexion brightened up or wrinkles diminished, but at 54 I don't look too bad. It is funny. People with swollen legs are told not to drink so much fluids and to stay away from salt, but I did the opposite and my legs are just about down to normal. I can wear cowboy boots again. I haven't worn cowboy boots since I was 42 or 44 years old. That's when my gout got really bad. It was pill after pill until I ended up with ulcers from them.

Now I don't take any pills. My joint pain is just about gone. It'll flare up now and again. It's the kind of work that I do. It depends on the stress, especially in the shoulders. I do a lot of heavy work, a lot of pulling, picking up heavy tires and parts. It's all I do all day. Some days you go home and your shoulders hurt, but that's from normal wear and tear.

Before I started on "The Water Cure," on a scale from one to ten, I felt like checking in, a zero. I wanted to die, but now, at least, I am a seven or eight. When I get to ten, I'll let you know.

Arthritis: A Final Word

From all of the arthritis testimonials you have read, it should now be obvious that the orthodox medical perception of arthritis is a grave error. That's because the pain is viewed as the problem, and all efforts are directed at eliminating the pain. The truth is that the pain is an alarm signal that dehydration is present and needs to be corrected immediately, or the damage will continue and the pain will get worse.

Some swimming pools have an alarm that signals a switch to run more water into the pool. Once the water level reaches its proper level, the flow is shut off.

If, instead of taking pain medication for the pain caused by lack of water in our joints, we just drank water and added a little sea salt, the pain would soon go because the nutritional needs of the joints have been addressed. You could have accomplished the same thing just by taking a swim in the ocean, where the water and sea salt needs of your body would also be addressed.

For more scientific information, go to watercure.com and read the scientific information, or purchase Dr. Batmanghelidj's book, *"Your Body's Many Cries for Water,"* for the rest of the story.

CHAPTER THREE: DEPRESSION

Introduction, by Bob Butts

L earn how simply the cause of depression can be eliminated - at no cost.

As in many other illnesses, dehydration is a major factor in cases of depression. Depression is a common but serious illness. Most people get rid of depression in two to four days once dehydration is corrected.

> **Message from Bob Butts:** I strongly suggest that anyone with depression pick up Dr. B.'s book, "Obesity, Cancer, Depression," and read pages 89 through 97 to completely understand how simple depression is to cure. If you live in Northeastern Pennsylvania, stop in at any Cee-Kay Auto Store and borrow the book with a deposit.

My personal experience with people with depression has been that it has been incredibly simple to cure when the cause is eliminated: chronic dehydration. It is about as simple to cure as brown grass. My favorite story is when I was invited to give a Water Cure lecture to people whose depression was so bad they had to go for counseling full time. They could not even hold a job. This counseling center was in the Scranton-Wilkes-Barre area in Pennsylvania. The reason my wife and I were invited there was because a nurse, Marilyn Fox, who got rid of MS by using the Water Cure, recommended it.

We had only one hour to talk to the patients and the counselors. My first question was, "What do you drink?" The response was coffee, tea, alcohol and soda. In fact , most were drinking a caffeinated soda while we talked to them. The only time they drank water was with their pills.

I then asked them to tell me all their illnesses. There were many, and all were related to dehydration. One had something we never heard of before called agoraphobia, which made it impossible for her to be close to people, drive a car or go shopping. She also asked if the Water Cure could help that, too.

We told her that we know it will cure her asthma, but we didn't know about the phobia. If they can't have salt, I suggest that they ask their doctor to give them a saline IV.

Meanwhile, the lady with the agoraphobia, after just two days on the Water Cure, drove her mother to the King of Prussia mall near Philadelphia without a hitch and no trace of depression or any problem being in a crowd of people. Every one of the patients of the counseling center was 100% free of depression in three weeks, and all were discharged. We were never allowed back because we got rid of all of their customers.

As you can see, the people at the counseling center were never mentally depressed. Their dietary deficiencies caused depression symptoms. Because our nation is addicted to money, it is almost impossible for anyone to expose solutions that will eliminate the sources of our income.

I think that 90% of people with depression can be cured as simply as these people were. What is extremely important is not to blame anyone, because it is the culture of corruption in our nation that screwed us up.

So long as we remain addicted to money, we have made it impossible to get rid of any high profit problem. See if you can find one single person who will support a free solution to the problem that is their source of income.

Testimonials: The following testimonials are from victims of depression who have found the "Water Cure."

Carlos Howard

I would just like to let you know that I have been experiencing symptoms that are given the label of depression for about six months. On the same day that I began to increase my water intake from 72 ounces per day to 155 ounces per day (I didn't even take any sea salt), every symptom that I had disappeared.

> **Message from Bob Butts:** Not taking the sea salt is dangerous, as you will lose your electrolytes.

I am a current college student and I have decided to change my major to nursing, because what I will do for the rest of my life is help people with the Water Cure who are suffering needlessly. I have watched and listened to all of the downloads on watercure2.org and I plan to buy all of Dr. B.'s books and memorize them.

Richard

Hi, I want to take moment to share my experience with the Water Cure. My name is Richard, living in New York City. I was suffering from extreme anxiety, panic attacks, etc. I started the program, and have since noticed a big difference in my stress levels (I'm much calmer) as well as higher energy levels and overall sense of well being. I've dropped a good 20 pounds as well! I was, however, still dealing with frequent urination, having to urinate every 30 minutes or so. I would also notice some ups and downs with my day-to-day feelings, some days feeling quite good while other days having a return of some of the old anxiety.

For the past few weeks or so, Jim Bolen has been suggesting to me to try a bagel and then drink water with salt. This, Jim explained, should help keep the water in the body for at least two hours, and allow the water enough time to top off the still somewhat dehydrated cells.

After a few weeks of my resisting trying the bagels (for fear of putting on excess weight), I tried my first bagel yesterday at 4:00, followed by 16 ounces of water and a little sea salt. I did not urinate until 7:30!!! I then had dinner at eight again with one whole bagel and 16 ounces of water/salt. I then did not urinate until 11:00!!!

To top it off, I slept the entire night without awakening one time to urinate. A first in 20 years!!!! If you are dealing with frequent urination, I urge you to try Jim Bolen's advice. Eat a bagel with your water/salt. A.K.A. The Magic Bullet!!! Thank you, Jim!!!!

Olivia Lennon, olivialennon@bigpond.com
I am 47 years old and have been on the water and salt cure for just over a month. I am feeling so much better. My depression lifted after two weeks, and my hot flashes have just about disappeared (after spending hundreds of dollars on menopause treatment).

Just thought I'd give you an update on the progress of the Water Cure treatment. I have now been drinking two liters of water per day and adding 3/4 teaspoon Celtic sea salt to my meals for just over two months, including a daily intake of vitamin B6, which Dr. Batmanghelidj suggests for hot flashes. I am also eating a lot more fresh fruit and vegetables, plus nuts and seeds. My depression and mood swings, which I suffered for a couple of years, have gone. My hot flashes have greatly reduced. I am not taking any drug of any kind, and feel wonderful. I have also noticed my skin is much softer. I am sleeping much better and feel more relaxed in general.

I would like to say a BIG THANK YOU for supporting Dr. Batmanghelidj, and for your watercure2 website. I have started sharing Water Cure with my family and will certainly share this with people I come in contact with.

Tina, phg@speed4me.de
Hello. My name is Tina. I am a 37-year-old mother of four. My children are 11, 9, 7, and 3. We live a very healthy life in Germany's Black Forest. I always gave water to my children. I never bought lemonade and other soft drinks.

After I nursed my little one until she was one year old, I became very depressed, suffered from PMS, and felt very miserable. I am a jogger, and I began to cry during jogging more and more often. I even had thoughts of running away and leaving my family.

During this time, I felt the problem was physical, not in my head. My body missed something, but I couldn't tell what. At this time, I was drinking almost no water, only black tea.

One day last Fall, I went to a lecture about the pH level in the body and learned about the negative effects of caffeine. I decided to stop drinking black tea. I began drinking decaffeinated green and herbal tea, and taking vitamins and supplements as a nutritional friend suggested: zinc citrate, guarana yams, OPC tablets, carotin tablets, lecithin, Super B caps, and aloe vera caps. I felt better very fast. I decided to also remove my hormonal spiral, which made me have no menstrual bleeding. I have my normal period again, and it makes me feel better, too.

Two weeks ago I discovered your books and your wonderfully simple theory about water. Suddenly everything makes sense to me - my having four children, nursing them every time for one year, jogging, and not drinking!

My body missed water - just simple water! Wow!

Courtney Diddle, Kansas City, Missouri
Dear Dr. Batmanghelidj:

I just became aware of your book, *"Your Body's Many Cries for Water."* I will be forever grateful for your years of research in reference to the role of water in the functioning of the human body. The chapter in the book pertaining to depression was the solution to over ten years of struggle in my life.

In your book, your simple formula for drinking water at the rate of a minimum of two quarts (64 oz. = 8 glasses) per day plus salt of a half teaspoon over a 24-hour period has been the answer for my depression. Because of my weight, I follow the additional suggested formula of half the body weight number in ounces of water required to properly keep the cells fully hydrated (200 pounds body weight = 100 ounces of water required). I make sure I ingest at least 3/4 teaspoon of table salt with my food during the same 24-hour period.

> **Message from Bob Butts:** Must be sea salt or you will be mineral-deficient.

I am a 68-year-old retired professional chemical engineer. I had battled depression symptoms from 1985 to 1995. My wife, a nurse clinician, passed away in 1984. I was forced into early retirement after 33-1/2 years with a major oil company in 1985. Those familiar with the role of high stress causing dehydration, as in Figure 9 in your book, will understand my problem. In addition, I had bought into the idea that a low fat diet was the way to good health. Thus, all the factors were in place for my body to show symptoms of depression.

What I know now is that most of the anti-depressants used to treat patients with depression are also diuretics. I always manifested the symptom of extreme dry mouth sensation after being placed on anti-depressants. The *symptom of anxiety* then comes forth because of the additional need for water by the body. Add a prescribed anti-anxiety pill and the patient (me) was on a chemical teeter totter trying to achieve a balance of a normal life.

Plus, in the Physicians Desk Reference (PDR), in the listing for the above medications is the nice word, suicide. I have struggled when on anti-depressants and anti-anxiety medication with the fleeting surges of the mind wanting to die. However, I never had the courage to act out the desire. The ultimate solution that worked for me, water and salt was the simple answer.

In summary, for over a year I have been free of the need to take any medication of any kind. In December, I qualified with no medical restrictions for a Class 111 physical for a private pilot's license. In addition, my annual eye check revealed that my eye peripheral vision had improved relative to previous annual tests. My belief is that the cells in the eye have become better hydrated. I can read without glasses.

May the value of your research and protocol continue to spread and be understood.

Jeffrey Wilkins

Dear Dr. Batmanghelidj:

I am writing to comment on and express my thank you for your research and your book, *"Your Body's Many Cries for Water."* I found it very concise and logical in its presentation and helpful in its message. I would also like to relay my experience prior to reading your book and the implementation of drinking more water.

I have no physical illness that I am aware of and enjoy good health. Yet, for all of my adult life I struggled with depression states. These states are not predictable, and I have found little effective remedy other than simply to endure and wait.

Without describing my depression, I can say that for me it was often near debilitating, and I have as a consequence done considerable experimentation in an effort to find relief. I have tried numerous therapies, both additive and subtractive.

In the additive, I have tried acupuncture, homeopathy, Chinese herbs, western herbs, chiropractic, sound and color therapy, chemical drugs, vitamins, essential oils, more light, colon-cleansing, ozone and oxygen supplements, meditation, individual and group psychotherapy, macrobiotic diet, and more exercise.

In the subtractive, I have eliminated amalgam fillings, caffeine, meat, and sugar, alcohol, drugs and all foods during certain periods in my life.

In regard to the effects of these trials, I can say that only the increasing exposure to natural sunlight, and use of antidepressant chemical drugs have had a noticeable effect on my depression. I still get more sunlight, but have abandoned drugs due to unacceptable side effects and concerns over long term dependency.

I read *"Your Body's Many Cries for Water"* nearly three months ago and started drinking at least eight glasses a day of water two months ago. I think that after this time I can, with relative certainty, say that there has been a marked improvement in my mood and absence of depressive states. This I say as a general statement. There are times when I feel low, but on the whole I feel much improved. I have much more humor and my thoughts are much more optimistic. I have observed that, even a single day without drinking water has a negative effect. I feel compelled to thank you for your work and for bringing it to the public, although I cannot comment on the relationship between drinking more water and other maladies.

I would not hesitate to recommend the book and the practice of drinking more water to anyone who struggles with depression.

John J., **Falls Church, Virginia**
Dr. F. Batmanghelidj:

Thank you so very much for your book, *"Your Body's Many Cries for Water.* It has radically changed my life for the better. As a registered nurse, I was at first skeptical, but tried it. An inmate can do very little for themselves to obtain medical care.

Prison health services are not generally very high quality, nor easy to access when needed.

> **Message from Bob Butts:** Prisons are notorious for banning salt. This causes countless problems.

The new paradigm relating to water is wonderful medicine. When I first inquired about the book, I was in severe pain from both my kidneys and lower intestines. My urinary output was very low, only urinating small amounts twice a day. The urine was concentrated and dark. My bowels were chronically constipated.

Initially, I started with 60 to 70 ounces of water per day. This helped some, but not so much as I had hoped. After increasing my water intake to 120 to 150 ounces per day, I have found that it has relieved the pains and increased urine output to normal. As an added blessing, my mental attitude has also greatly improved. I had been sad, withdrawn and chronically tired. Now I have more energy, and inner peace, and my mental outlook is better. It has become a brighter day for me without the pains, worry over an illness, and to find mental peace.

I have spread word of your work and the water treatment to my friends, family, and the health service staff. Some have embraced your teachings. Those who do not have been challenged to try it and see.

"It costs nothing to go to the tap and get a drink." Your good health is worth eight glasses of water.

Thank you again for your work and kindness towards me.

Depression: A Final Word

Few people, other than those who have suffered with depression for years, can appreciate what it is like to get rid of this monster called depression, whose solution is so simple. I beg all who got well using Dr. B.'s discovery to do all that you can to tell the world. The entire world must know what Dr. B. did and the sacrifices he made for humanity.

Keep his book, "Obesity, Cancer, Depression," by your bed so you never forget what this man did for you. I want the whole world to know how it feels when they help someone get well by passing on to them Dr. B.'s greatest health discovery in history, the Water Cure.

Every time you help someone get well, the better you will feel, and the happier you will be. Nothing will bring you more joy.

–Bob Butts

CHAPTER FOUR: HEART DISEASE

Introduction

> The following article has been chosen to serve as the introduction to this chapter, since we could not have said it better.

Family Practice News: Drinking a Lot of Water Sinks Fatal Heart Attack Risk, by Barbara Baker

In a study of more than 34,000 Seventh Day Adventists - people who have been followed for six years - drinking at least eight glasses of water a day was associated with a significantly decreased risk of fatal coronary heart disease among those without CHD, stroke or diabetes at baseline. Jacqueline Chan, PhD, reported on this at the 20th Congress of the European Society of Cardiology.

In a separate presentation, her associate, Dr. Synnove F. Knutsen, reported that among those with a history of CHD, stroke or diabetes at baseline, drinking at least five glasses of water a day substantially lowered the risk of fatal stroke. Both investigators are epidemiologist at Loma Linda (California) University.

Blood viscosity and hematocrit have previously been shown to be risk factors for heart disease and stroke. "We believe that good hydration has a positive impact on these risk factors," Dr. Knutsen said in an interview. News media and mainstream medicine ignore this.

Testimonials: The following testimonials are from victims of heart disease who have been helped by the Water Cure.

Norbert Lynham, norbert23@myway.com

I am a retired racing cyclist (not quite at the level of Lance Armstrong). So, I know what the top level of fitness feels like. Eight years ago I went through a period of great stress. My wife developed cancer and suffered greatly for nine months before she died. This took its toll on my health. I developed a number of serious health problems, including three heart attacks over the next two years. The health providers in England told me they could not help as I was not suitable for any bypass or heart replacement at my age. They also advised that they considered that I would not survive another attack. This news was a great shock.

I then took time to consider how I could turn this around. If the medical world had failed me, it was time for me to control my health, something I should have been doing all along. A former business partner talked to me about my water intake and how important it was. During my racing years I was aware of this and always drank water both before and during my race. How could I have been so stupid as to forget this simple rule?

I decided to start a new life in Spain and my business partner gave me a book as a small leaving present. Dr. Batmanghelidj's book, *"Your Body's Many Cries for Water."* After reading it, I was blown away. The path back to health lay there in this book. I visit www.watercure2.org two or three times a week to see how things are going. My doctor here in Spain (a heart man) tells me all is fine, blood pressure being normal and my resting heart rate being 60, which he says is great for a man aged 77.

When I started the Water Cure program, I soon found that there was a lot more to it than having the correct intake of water and sea salt. You need to understand what happens when you neglect to drink the water. This is a must if you hope to get positive results. Many people tell me they do drink a lot of water. What they don't tell me is the large amounts of fluids they take that dehydrate them. They think of these fluids as containing water. So, to me this shows a lack of understanding of the basics.

Now to the protocol I used to get positive results. I soon understood that if this was going to work, I had to get as much information as possible to help along the way. Dr. B's book, *"Your Body's Many Cries for Water,"* is, I feel, a *must!* From this you will get a better understanding of the subject. You will need a level of support as you progress. Here I found the watercure2.org site... my Bible. I found the level of information invaluable. Be aware that there is no fixed program to follow.

I have made some adjustments to the program that fit my own conditions and environment. If you are ill or elderly, start off slowly, say half of the recommended amount of water, until you start to hydrate. Water must stay in the body if it is going to have any effect. You should not have to visit the loo (bathroom) for about two hours after drinking your ration of water. As I mentioned above, help in sorting out these issues is available on the web site watercure2.org.

Important points to remember:

- Don't expect immediate results. It will require time and effort. Cut out all or as many dehydrating drinks as possible. Diet and daily exercise are also important. Look closely at these points.

- The correct amount of sleep, I feel, is also important. Your body needs time to recover from the stress we put on it daily.

- Water intake must be adjusted constantly, depending on the level of activity, temperature, etc.

Here in Spain, good quality food is widely available. Also, when I tasted our local tap water, I found the pH to be 7.5. As well as the amount of water we drink, I feel that the quality is also very important. Being unsure as to other contaminants that may be in our tap water, I installed an effective four-stage filter unit.

In Spain, during July and August, temperatures rise to 37 to 40 degrees. I have lifted my water intake to four liters a day and also the amount of salt to just over half of a teaspoon.

So, to finish, remember you will have to put a lot of time and effort into it to get results. If you do, I can assure you it will be well worthwhile. There is little value in getting old if poor health is spoiling your enjoyment of life.

After four years following the Water Cure, I am now off all of the cocktail of drugs I was taking and feel great. I am a member of a retired activities club. The wife of the club chairman has asked me to give a talk to the members on the Water Cure. I am not sure about this as most people I tell about it think I am nuts! I would dearly like to spread the word, so any advice you could offer would be of great help. It makes me mad to see how the public is being denied this information. At the beginning of this year I invested in a new road race bike (vanity), which I now use for a morning spin every day. I am now back in control of my health, which has to be good for a 77-year-old.

I was so lucky to have a friend who provided me with the book that led me back to health. Please! Please! Keep up the great work you are doing. A million thanks to all involved.

Samuel K. Liguori, Program Director, WARD Broadcasting, Pittston, PA

Dear Dr. Balmanghelidj:

Just a short letter to thank you for informing our listeners about the health benefits of drinking two quarts of water a day.

Not only did you help our radio audience, but I personally have enjoyed a resurgence of energy after drinking two quarts of water each day for just over one week. The angina pain that I endured over five years has disappeared, and the distress from a hiatal hernia has greatly lessened. I feel like a new person.

I've done talk shows at WARD Radio for the past 20 years, and I must say your interview with us is one I'll always remember.

[See his interview on the WYOU water cure documentary on www.watercure2.org]

Anonymous

> I'm sending a testimonial without any names. For now, we're letting friends and family think my husband is taking his meds. I could add that your coaching was crucial. It made him feel that someone believed in this program besides his wife. I wasn't sure if you want your name in it, but we will be forever grateful to you. If there is anything you think I have left out below, I will be happy to fix it.
> –Sharon

My husband is 80 years old and had a six-way heart bypass four years ago. He recovered very quickly from the surgery and felt so good he stopped taking the medications the doctors had prescribed. He was very healthy for four years, not even getting the flu in the winter like everyone else around us. However, this Spring, three months ago, he had difficulty getting his breath. It was so severe we rushed him to the emergency room.

He was in the hospital for about three days, where they diagnosed him with having congestive heart failure, water on the lungs, diabetes, high blood pressure, and high cholesterol, besides being low on potassium. His cardiologist became irate when he realized my husband hadn't bothered to get a primary care physician and had stopped taking the meds a few months after his surgery. They sent him home with prescriptions for Glyburide and Metformin for diabetes, Lasix as a diuretic, Lipitor and Carveditol for his heart, besides Potassium. The doctor was so mean and rude, my husband fired him. However, the new doctor he got was just as adamant about meds, salt-free diet, no sweets, and no herbs or vitamins... except for vitamin C!

We struggled for about two months with trying to follow the strict regulations for a diabetic and heart patient, eating a small, tasteless balanced meal six times a day. Some days he felt pretty good, and other days felt like an invalid with blood sugar fluctuating up and down.

He couldn't pull a weed without getting short of breath, and certainly couldn't carry anything like a stick of wood for the fireplace. Some days he could barely make it from his recliner to the bathroom. I thought for sure I was going to be a widow. I noticed his skin seemed dry and I was concerned about the water pill he was ordered to take, because we know the importance of water.

I found the Water Cure web site and we read the information there. However, we were concerned about water coming back into his lugs and didn't understand why it happened in the first place. The doctors told us it was because he hadn't taken the medication they prescribed.

After reading testimonials about other people with congestive heart failure getting well, we decided to give it a try because we already knew that our bodies, if given the right building blocks to work with, can regenerate themselves. When we began drinking water and eating salt, things began to change in three days. My husband stopped all the meds and just started concentrating on eating foods like potatoes with skins, eggs, pudding, ice cream, orange juice, chicken, green beans, salads, cheese while taking chlorophyll, multi vitamins, and flaxseed oil.

At this writing, it has been eleven days and what a change! When we walk, I want to yell. "Wait for me!' is what I have to shout to him. He feels great and can carry heavy things.

This, I believe, was my husband's mistake. Last winter was cold and he didn't get out and walk and exercise as usual. However, every morning he got up early, drove to the coffee shop, and swigged a huge strong cup of coffee. In the winter, people forget to drink water because they don't feel hot and thirsty. With help from the coffee that is a diuretic, he totally dehydrated himself. Therefore, water collected in his lungs because his body was short of water.

Because I was restricting the salt from our diet as the doctor ordered, I got dehydrated, too. I spend quite a bit of time on my computer and, by bedtime, my eyes usually really hurt. With more water, I read a book all afternoon, and in the evening worked on the computer, and my eyes felt fine. Like my husband, I have more energy, too.

Message from Bob Butts: A man came into my store (CeeKay Auto) to tell me how his dad achieved a miracle after listening to how his son got rid of asthma and allergies after going on the Water Cure. His dad was in a hospital waiting to die after nine heart attacks. He had no hope. But he decided to try the Water Cure anyway. Then his son got a call from the hospital telling him that his dad had gone. He thought his dad had died. But he hadn't. But he was gone. He took his walker and walked out of the hospital and hitched a ride to his home. He would not go back, but two years later his then 82-year-old father married a 58-year-old woman. As of September 2010, he is 84 years old and is still doing great. I asked him for a full testimonial, which I haven't yet received.

David L.

My doctor told me that, if I didn't have a bypass operation, I'd have one year to live. That was in September 1996. I was persuaded not to have the operation after the best customer that I had, through the livestock business, Charlie, died after having a five-way bypass in New Jersey by the best doctors that money could buy. He got a blood clot. It was the 11th of November of 1996 that they buried Charlie. I made up my mind right then and there that I was not going to get a bypass surgery. Live or die, there was going to be no bypass.

I fought the doctors all along because I didn't believe I had a heart attack. I still don't, but they put me through all of the tests and they said I did in fact have one. But I got lucky about six months ago when I ran into Bob Butts. We sat there and talked. Bob walked me to the car and saw a bottle of Pepsi on the seat. I was the kind of person who drank eight to ten cases of Pepsi a week. Bob talked me into trying the Water Cure, and I went home shaking my head, but I said "What have I got to lose? You try it and it doesn't work, then you can go back to the Pepsi!"

Well, *I* tried it and five days later I felt better than I have in the last seven years. I don't understand how anything can help that quickly, but it did. I get up in the morning and I'm ready to go. I haven't had any problems that I know of since I started the Water Cure. I had an appointment with my doctor, and when he finished with my physical he looked at me and said, "I don't know what the heck you're doing, but don't stop."

I have been adding salt to my food as well. I went to the pharmacy in Moscow, Pennsylvania, and talked to the pharmacist, Eric Pussay, and he said, "Dave, I have the tapes and the books by Dr. Batmanghelidj and I don't see anything wrong with it." I told Eric they're going to put you out of business, and he said, "No way. People are too stupid to believe this."

Back in September, on a scale of one to ten, ten being the best, I felt like a five or six. They put me on heart medicine, monitored it, and did all the things I guess they have to do, but they really didn't convince me that I had heart trouble until they came in with a machine. They put it on my chest and when they turned it on it sounded like a washing machine working.

They told me that was my heart. An operator explained what was on the screen. He told me that 's where the damage is and that's when I finally believed it did happen. Here we are thirteen months later and on a scale of one to ten, I feel like a nine or ten. I have a very strong sense of well being.

I feel great and I do everything I want to do. I want to add that if there is anybody out there who thinks that this is crazy and it can't work, try it! Four or five days is all I will say to you. If you don't feel better in that time, then you probably aren't doing what Dr. Batmanghelidj says. I had a drought condition in my body.

Heart Attack: A Final Word

By reading these heart testimonials, I hope you now realize that the problem was never with your heart. You just didn't supply your body with the raw materials it needs to repair itself. *You were thirsty!*

> **Mayo Clinic tells how to prevent heart attacks with water**
> According to Mayo Clinic experts, the risk of a winter heart attack is at least 30% higher in the first few hours after waking. "After a long night's rest, most of us are quite dehydrated, which makes blood sticky and can trigger dangerous blood clots," explains Richard M. Fleming, M.D., medical director of the Fleming Heart and Health Institute in Omaha, Nebraska. Fortunately, you can easily erase the risk by drinking an eight-ounce glass of water within 15 minutes of waking.

CHAPTER FIVE: CANCER

Introduction

> Dr. Dean Burk's article serves as a fitting introduction to this section. Dr. Burk is an original founder of the National Cancer Institute.

"The more people making a living off of cancer, the more impossible it is to get rid of it"

This landmark study suggests something that most doctors, even oncologists, would never consider: that cancer can go away on its own. Typically, when this happens, it's brushed off as a fluke. But the new study found that even invasive cancers may go away without treatment, and it may happen more often than anyone thought.

The problem with cancer often lies not only with ignoring these health principles, but with the invasive and highly risky treatments that conventional medicine relies on to treat it - surgery, chemotherapy, and radiation. The alarming rates of cancer deaths across the world (cancer has a mortality rate of 90%, according to Italian oncologist Dr. Tullio Simoncini) speak volumes about the effectiveness or lack thereof, of these treatments. Yet, they are still regarded as the gold standard of cancer cure.

Chemotherapy is a classic example of a cure that is worse than the disease. In fact, many experts now say that cancer patients are more likely to die from cancer treatments than from the cancer itself.

"The majority of the cancer patients in this country die because of chemotherapy, which does not cure breast, colon or lung cancer. This has been documented over a decade and, nevertheless, doctors still utilize chemotherapy to fight these tumors," said Dr. Allen Levin, M.D., author of "*The Healing of Cancer.*"

> **Message from Bob Butts:** The truth is that cancer is no more a disease than brown grass is... both are caused by lack of water, and no drug or procedure can cure either. Read Dr. Batmanghelidj's incredible book, "*Obesity, Cancer, and Depression: Their Common Cause and Natural Cure.*"

Report from Bob Butts

A crying Moosic CeeKay auto employee on about October first, 2009, told us that her mom has breast cancer and was going to do the Water Cure immediately and also take chemo and radiation. Two weeks later, after going on the Water Cure, she told us her mom's prominent Scranton oncologist, while checking the status of her cancer, said that all traces of her mom's cancer were gone, and she had not even started the chemo and radiation, and she never did. She remained cancer-free. *(Throughout this book you will read many stories of speedy results.)*

Two weeks later, a foot doctor told me he has a number of Water Cure stories, including a patient who was under treatment for prostate cancer that was continuing to get worse. He went on the Water Cure and in two weeks the tumor shrunk 25%. This doctor's office has free Water Cure information displayed.

> **Message from Bob Butts:** I thank God for the more and more Northeastern Pennsylvania doctors who are telling patients about the Water Cure, calling the proof "undeniable." Ask your doctors what they think? You can also view incredible Water Cure news specials on watercure2.org, Youtube, and Facebook. Free CDs and loaner books are available at CeeKay Auto. See "Resources" in back matter of this book.

Testimonials: The following testimonials are from victims of cancer, who have found the Water Cure.

Jean Hale, jandjh@asop.ed.za

Just writing to say I started the Water Cure on 3/12/2009 following a lumpectomy of a lump in my right breast. It has been confirmed as a low-grade invasive carcinoma. Axillary glands (ten) were negative. The tumor was 13mm in size.

I came home from the hospital on 3/12/2009 and, by Divine Providence, found your web site, downloaded the diet, and commenced immediately together with the suggested supplements. I am feeling well, energized and sleeping well.

Last night, reading some of the conditions reported to have improved in others, I came across mention of the depigmentation of the skin (Vitiligo). I have had this on both of my forearms for several years, easily observed by others.

Well, I checked them there and then. There are two very small spots still showing the depigmentation. It is clearly on its way back to normal! Therefore, I am concluding that every other cell and function in my body is doing the same thing.

In addition, a small growth on my forehead at the hairline is becoming smaller and smaller.

I am confident of a full return to health and am not going to be agreeing with Tamoxifen or radiation treatment if it is suggested on Friday, 8/1/09, when I go for a follow-up check. I am sure my body and its immune system can heal itself as it was designed to do.

Thank you for the encouragement you are spreading.

Forum participant: www.watercure2.org web site

My lung cancer is gone!

I started the Water Cure in January after my doctors sent me home to die. I was diagnosed with stage four non-small-cell lung cancer. I had tumors in both lungs and it had spread to my colon, bones and prostate. I've been through the ringer: Chemo, Radiation, and Iressa. Nothing was helping. After my insurance ran out, I had to sell my home. These ******s took me for every penny I had and just left me to die.

A friend told me about this web site and said he had just lost one of his best friends to cancer, and that I should give it a try. All I can say is IT WORKS!!!!!

Yesterday I got my results back from the doctor, and my cancer is gone. My prostate is back to normal, and I can't believe my sex drive. I don't understand how it works, but it does. Thank you all. There's really nothing more I can say. I'm telling all of my friends about this site and I can only pray they'll listen. Tommy, if you read this, thank you, again, from the bottom of my heart. I've lost your phone number, so if you see this, please call me.

Focus Group Leader Response

That's awesome, Robert :-)!! But you did all of the work. I just found the site. I didn't start the Water Cure when I told you about it. But I did start it last month and no longer have problems with C.O.P.D. I'm healed as well :-)!!

Good luck, and don't forget to share this web site with as many people as you can. My phone number is on my web site under "contact us." I haven't had many Focus Groups because of my illness. I'm much better now, and I have a long road ahead of my trying to promote my web site without any money. I've been sick for so long that I don't know if I'll be able to make a comeback. But, when I do, I'll have a lot of focus groups to send you to. I wish us both the best of luck as well as the best of health.

Stephen James, Gold Coast, Australia

Thank you for your web site. My mum, aged 66, has been a Christian for 18 years. She was diagnosed with bowel and liver cancer last year on February fifth. She started a new course of cancer drugs, which cost $10,000, but because they were trial drugs they would not cost her anything if she agreed to go on them. The government would pay. My mum lives in New Zealand, and I live in Australia, so as you could imagine, I felt upset that I could not be with her through this time.

In September 2005, I took the three kids and my wife to see her for three weeks. She had lost a lot of weight, and was very slow to move. She had peeling feet and hands from her drugs, which made showering very painful. She also had uncontrollable diarrhea. I came away from visiting her angry, and knew that these drugs were not going to heal her.

Once back in Australia, I started a search on alternate cures. I was shocked on the amount of so-called cures. I did not know where to start. I came across several interesting sites about pH levels, and then a link came up about your site. I read several articles on your site and decided to buy a couple of Dr. B.'s books. After reading them, I phoned my mum to explain to her about Dr. B.'s Water Cure, but it seemed to fall on deaf ears. For several months I was receiving mum's blood results, and her liver function test was high but stable.

About June of this year, Mum started to feel pressure in her lower back, and went and had a blood test and scan. Things were getting worse. My mum asked the doctor if she had the full zone chemotherapy, how long would she live. The doctor said, "Two months if you do have it, and the same if you don't."

She decided to have the chemo, but after one dose of IV chemo, she was so sick that she decided to stop all treatment. Two weeks later my sister rung me and said mum has given up and wants to die. I decided to fly back to New Zealand and talk to her about the Water Cure again.

I arrived in New Zealand on the 22nd of July at 12:45 am. I was staying with my parents. As I came into the house, my mum called for me, and I was shocked to see my mum in a frail condition. She had not been out of bed for several days. I kissed her and said "I love you." As I tried to sleep that night, I thought, "How am I going to get her to try the Water Cure?"

The next morning I spoke to her again, and said "What have you got to lose?" I asked Mum her weight. She said around 60kg. She said, "I will try it." I found a 500ml bottle and said she had to drink three of these a day with 1/4 teaspoon of 80 mineral sea salt per lt.

The first day she took her full quota, but did not pass urine at all. I stopped the salt for one day, but continued her 1.5 lts. She started to pass urine, so I started the salt once more.

The third day, to everyone's surprise, Mum got out of bed and came down to the sitting room, and sat with us all. You should have seen my dad's face. Mum sat up for several hours that day.

Day four, Mum once again got up, drinking her salt water , and starting knitting my wife a scarf. Mum said, "I feel good."

Day five, Mum once again got up and sat with us all.

My sister came around and asked me if I would like to go to the shopping mall. Mum asked if she could go, too. That statement left us all speechless for a moment. So, away we all went to the mall. Mum walked with us for about 20 minutes around the mall.

I spoke to her more about the Water Cure the next few days that I was there. Mum said she was never a water drinker, and never used salt. My dad, who loves salt on everything, has low BP, and mum also has high BP and is on tablets for it.

Well, its now coming to the end of August 2006, and Mum is up every day, and goes shopping with Dad. I spoke to her on the phone yesterday and even her tone of voice is sharp. My mum has had a lot of prayer, and we know that Jesus went about teaching, preaching and healed people. And He is the same yesterday, today and forever. So, what He did yesterday, He will do today.

But, also, we reap what we sow.

> Moses 4:8, My people are destroyed for lack of knowledge.

Thanks, Bob, for giving us something to work with.

Dr. Lorraine Day (An internationally-acclaimed orthopedic trauma surgeon, world-known AIDS expert, and best-selling author.)

"You have Cancer. You're going to die!" the doctors told me. "But they were wrong!" says Lorraine Day, M.D. She was diagnosed with invasive breast cancer and had a lumpectomy of a small tumor. But the tumor soon recurred, became very aggressive, and grew rapidly.

Yet, Dr. Day rejected standard therapies because of their destructive side effects, and because those therapies often lead to death. She chose instead to rebuild her immune system using the natural, simple, inexpensive therapies designed by God and available to everyone so the body could heal itself.

"Dr. Batmanghelidj's discovery regarding water was critical to my recovery. I could not have recovered without it."

–Lorraine Day, M.D.

Andrew J. Bauman, IV (most recent update)
Scranton, Pennsylvania, drew4HD@aol.com

I became 42 years old in October 1998. In 1995, I was urged to "get my affairs in order" and to "pull out all stops" by a hermatologist/Oncologist from a prominent local hospital. Cutaneous B-Cell Lymphoma was the diagnosis. Number 15 in a list of medical challenges including diabetes, hypertension, neuropathy, retinopathy, candida albicans (yeast), chronic fatigue, obesity, arthritis, bursitis, to name a few. I used to ask, "Why me?" Every square inch of my body tested positive for cancer. I was sent home to die. After the Water Cure, diet and exercise, I was 100% free of cancer and more.

Today, I know all of that led to many new doors in my life.

In the meantime, I needed tires for my car to be able to travel for my appointments to the many doctors I was seeing. Don't forget. I was challenged by diabetes and 13 other illnesses besides the cancer. The parts man at the counter at Cee-Kay Auto in Moosic, PA, began conversing with me and invited me upstairs to meet the owner of the business (Bob Butts). He told me about the "Water Cure." Was it just a coincidence that I was hearing about the importance of water and hydration once again? My college days and Biology courses were also now flashing again in my mind. My doctor stressed the importance of water. Now I believe that there are no coincidences, and that all things happen for a reason in God's plan. This was happening around October and November of 1995. Bob put me in touch with F. Batmanghelidj, M.D., discoverer or the Water Cure, who told me how to use it.

I began my treatments: started trying to drink a gallon of clean, pure, filtered water a day, changed my diet to a more whole grain with fresh fruits and vegetables regimen, took my supplements, and literally surrendered my fate into God's hands.

Well, I guess He planned on my writing this. In March of 1996, I was feeling somewhat better, and the specialist at the major hospital scheduled another Gallium scan. When I was in the office waiting for the results, he entered shaking his head. I could feel my pulse racing. He told me that either the machine malfunctioned now, or in my initial scan, because it seemed odd that I was glowing positive for cancer from head to toe only six months prior to this scan, and now there wasn't one cell testing positive for cancer in my entire body!

Those tears welling up in my eyes were joyful, as I thought of the children and loved ones at home, and my zeal to go to them with the news. The doctor and I talked about what my "Naturopath" and I had done, and agreed about the importance of water and salt. He said it was possible that I was very fortunate in finding the right combination that healed me.

How wonderful that all these years of "suffering," as our society calls it, were really revealing lessons learned ("miracles" or "shifts in my perceptions") - those proverbial "silver linings in every dark cloud." Yes. I am (reference to the Deity I AM. within my spirit intended) still overcoming some challenges with my health, yet now I am winning! By drinking more water, changing some perceptions, making dietary changes, supplementation and adding Alternative Medicine to the mix, I have a more balanced life and continue learning more each moment of each beautiful day, one at a time. People in hospitals recover when fluids - "intravenous salt water" - restores the natural balance so medicine and body treatments can begin the process of regeneration.

Update (ten years later) - Today, I am in New York City (since 9/3/01), nine years clean from cancer. I am still under the care of eight specialists for my various conditions. I continue to improve with all the chronic conditions I developed over 30 years of dehydration. At least now I see the light.

The specialists I see all remain amazed at my story and promise to refer patients to me as I begin my practice (Integrated Medicine). June 3, 2005, I graduated from Acupuncture College and September 2005 will begin a Chinese herbal program for Internal Medicine, working towards my eventual Doctorate Degree in Acupuncture and Oriental (herbal) Medicine.

After studying Asian Bodywork techniques and "Chinese" as well as "Bio" Medicines, I remain convinced of proper hydration with water and sea salt's role in facilitating healing as a basis for using other modalities successfully. May God bless Dr. Batmanghelidj's spirit and his family for the tireless efforts of reconnecting us with Hippocrates' roots in Modern Medicine.

May God Bless Bob and Connie Buts for their help and friendship and support in my journey, as well as for bringing Dr. B. into my life. Thank you to the many good souls, including all of the teachers who have blessed me.

Finally, thank you, God. You are my constant and abundant source of all there is that is good. I answer all emails and speak with people on the phone about this today. I would love to answer your questions and direct you toward sensible choices if you choose to contact me. *(Find the complete story on watercure2.org and Youtube.)*

Wells Jackson, Colorado Springs, Colorado

To: Dr. F. Batmanghelidj:

I am writing to thank you for leading me through the cure of prostate cancer. During a flight physical in July 1999, my PSA was at 4.6. I was referred to a urologist, which led to a biopsy that came back positive in October. I went to Walter Reed Medical Center for a second opinion in January 2000, where my PSA was found to be at 5.7, and it was confirmed as cancer.

While home for Christmas, my mother kept talking about your book, *"Your Body's Many Cries for Water."* I finally asked her to please stop talking about it so I could enjoy the holidays and my granddaughters, but I promised to read the material she gave me on the flight back to Germany.

While I was at Walter Reed in Washington, D.C., I found out all I could about possible cures and facilities or clinics that might serve as alternative resources, because everyone I talked to wanted to operate. Actually, three choices were recommended to me: wait and watch, radiation therapy, and surgery, which was their strongest recommendation.

I began drinking water while at Walter Reed as a result of downloading your volumes of information from the Internet at watercure.com. I emailed you because I had some questions, and when I returned to Europe, I found an answer from you inviting me to call you at your office, which I did. You asked me many questions and told me to begin drinking water, carrot juice, orange juice, use salt (which I had not done in twenty years), and lots of vegetables and fruits. The only eating restrictions you gave me was to not eat fried foods. You also told me to give up coffee, alcohol, and sodas. You told me to walk for an hour in the morning, and an hour at night... faithfully. You invited me to call you whenever I had questions and when I asked what it would cost, you stated there would be no charge... WOW!!!

Since then, I have called regularly, every week at first, and about once a month more recently. I have had monthly PSA tests run, and they generally have been within safe tolerance since February (the first month after beginning the Water Cure) In March, I went to Panama and Vietnam and was not able to follow the regimen faithfully, but I did keep drinking my daily amount of water, and my PSA was slightly elevated when it was tested in April. I went back to the regimen and the PSA was way down the next month.

I went to Panama for a family reunion in late July and early August, where I drank some beer and coffee, and when I returned to Europe, I found my PSA up again. This concerned me and I called to speak with you about it. In our conversation, you questioned me very closely about the consumption of alcohol, and I confessed that, since I live in Germany where the world's best beers are available, I usually had one or two at dinner. You told me not to drink any alcohol, and I obeyed.

You also shared with me that the high PSA indicated a higher acidity in my body and recommended that I eat lots of vegetables, particularly green ones, to cause a higher pH. The next month's test was at 3.3.

At first, when I attempted to explain to medical doctors what I am doing, they basically blew me off. But more recently, I have spoken to a few who are interested.

Since beginning this suggested regimen, I have really felt better than before I started. I was in pretty good shape, but within three weeks, I noticed that when I did the same cardio-vascular exercises as before, I had to work much harder to raise my heart beat to the normal 150 that I had always achieved before. It would only reach 130 with the same effort. I asked you about this, and you told me it was because my heart muscles were probably dehydrated before, and no longer have to work so hard. With the same effort now, I only achieved a heart rate of 115 to 120.

For years I have had some pains in my knees and in my hip when I walked or ran, and my knees hurt when I walked after getting up out of a chair. This was completely gone after about three months of water-drinking. My nagging lower back pain has disappeared, and I feel really great. I am 60 and quite frankly I feel about as good as I did at 40, and I am cured of prostate cancer.

I was raised on a farm, flew fighters, built houses and commercial buildings, and owned a number of construction businesses in my adult years so, from my experience, I am a practical thinker and water makes sense. I can personally claim that your information works, and it is amazing that so many other friends of mine think it is just too simple of a solution. It is particularly distressing to encounter the ignorance shown by traditional medical people, who seem to be blinded by their training and professional arrogance when it comes to acceptance of your information.

Thank you very much, Dr. Batmanghelidj, and I pray that "WE" are successful in getting your practical information heard by people who can benefit from it.

Please feel free to share this information with anyone it will benefit.

Carol Harrison, MsCrafty40@aol.com

Dear Bob Butts:

Thank you for lending the audio tapes to us. I was so grateful that my sister was able to pick them up for me and have the opportunity to meet you and speak with you and Connie. Tell Connie for me that I really do appreciate the angel statue, for I am a great collector of angels myself.

I am trying to listen to the tapes as much as I can throughout the day so I can return them to you as quicky as possible.

Lorraine Day is an excellent example in the powers of God. I hope that you understand, Bob, that I firmly believe that the Lord has taken over and is leading me in the right direction. My faith in God is stronger than this cancer, and I'm learning such vast amounts of information from the audios.

I knew from the first day of my daughter Elise's diagnosis that there were greater hands that would be involved in her cure. I handed this over to our Lord because, for a mom, it was too much to handle, and I have Faith and Trust in the Heavenly Father. He knows what he is doing. Then, by the graces of God, I found you and Connie and watercure2.org.

I am very grateful for your help and support, and most of all because you, Bob Butts, know something that others just don't get - that all good things come if we just listen with our hearts... that God whispers to us all the time and leads us in the right direction, if we would only listen. I'm hearing this message, Bob, and working diligently every day to open the hearts of others. But my first priority is to heal and cure my daughter. I think we are well on our way to understanding how to do that.

Elise is doing much better since starting on the water and Celtic salt. Both of the remaining tumors have shrunk down to a minimal size, and there are only two small clusters remaining in her bones. It is still a lot, but it is much better since watecure2.org. She is now much healthier and stronger, and I attribute that to becoming hydrated more and more every day.

Thanks so much for all of your help and guidance. God Bless You.

Patrick McVeigh, Floral Park, New York

Firstly, Bob, I want to thank you for your web site and for your unselfish dedication to Dr. Batmanghelidj and the Water Cure.

About five years ago, I was told by doctors - one at Sloan Kettering Memorial Cancer Center - that I had lymphoma (of the stomach lining). I went on a short water fast, and after four days vomited large amounts of bile. I continued for several more days and increased my water-drinking to about 80-100 ounces a day. I did not listen to the doctors and took no other treatment.

Today, I am in great health, all thanks to water. I only wish that I had learned the secret earlier in my life. Lymph is just about 90%+ water and no one should get lymphoma. It is all due to dehydration. I understand that you have a radio program. I don't believe it can be heard in New York. Is there any way that I can get to hear it?

> **Message from Bob Butts:** It can be heard on our site, watercure2. org, under Positive Press Radio. *(See section on pH in the back matter of this book.)*

Thank you, again, for your work. But I must wonder why it is so difficult to get people to listen and understand about the benefits of water.

Reverend Stan Moore, Word of Life Fellowship Church in Pembrook Pines, Florida

Reverend Moore said he found biblical truth in the Water Cure when he read 2nd Kings, second chapter, lines 19-22.

> **From 2nd Kings, 2nd chapter, lines 19-22.** 19: And the men of the city said unto Elisha, Behold, I pray thee, the situation of this city is pleasant, as my lord seeth, but the water is naught, and the ground barren. 20: And he said, Bring me a new cruse, and put salt therein. And they brought it to him. 21; And he went forth into the spring of the waters, and cast the salt in there, and said, Thus saith the LORD, I have healed these waters, there shall not be from hence any more death or barren land. 22: So the waters were healed unto this day, according to the saying of Elisha which he spoke.

After a church member was cured with terminal cancer because of the Water Cure, he informed his congregation about it. Upon hearing this, the wife of a man who was just prayed for because he was incurably ill with bone cancer and several other conditions, went to the hospital and they started giving him small amounts of water. His family was told there was no hope, and to accept his death. Six weeks later this man was totally well and gave his testimonial in church. That was at the end of August 2000.

The entire church pledged to follow the Water Cure for one year, and the results were immediate, as anyone with an understanding of water would expect. People were getting rid of all kinds of problems, many of which were called incurable. (Their address is 15610 SW 12th Street, Pembrook, Florida.).

Cancer: A Final Word

As you can see, cancer is similar to all of the other ills in this book. The real cause is dehydration.

CHAPTER SIX: HEADACHES

Introduction

A headache is defined as a pain in the head that is located above the eyes or the ears, behind the head (occipital), or in the back of the upper neck. It is one of the most common locations of pain in the body.

It has been determined by a Yahoo study that headaches are caused by dehydration.

Message from Bob Butts: That is 100% true.

A survey of victims of headaches resulted in answers that indicated that the increase in water consumption cured their headaches.

The Yahoo survey - and the testimonials below - provide points of reference for headache sufferers as they seek relief from the pain of headaches. But the bottom line is that most headaches will quickly disappear once the dehydration is corrected.

Testimonials: The following testimonials are from victims of headaches who have found the "Water Cure."

Alan G. Burley

Letter to Darrell Stoddard, darrellstoddard@gmail.com

I want to personally thank you for saving my life. There are very few good doctors with any integrity left. It is all about the money. I forgot if I got your website from Kevin Trudeau's book or Bottom Line Health. It does not really matter. It is only important that I found you.

Two years ago, it seemed as though it happened overnight, but my symptoms were gradually becoming more noticeable over time. Starting in my teens, I thought it was just old age creeping up on me. First it started with knee injuries, then my upper back and neck started really bothering me at 41 years of age. I had been in a car wreck five or six years prior to these symptoms. I thought it was the result of the wreck. Sometimes this does not show up for several years.

The headaches were miserable - always in my neck, back of the head and top of the head. It seemed like I went for a solid year and had a headache every day.

I went to Orthopedic, Chiropractor, Neurosurgeon, and General Doctor. I had an MRI done that stated that I had a mild bulging disk in my neck C6, slight herniating at T3 and T4, and a mild herniating at T8, T9;. T3 and T4 were off the machine. T6 was the worst of all as far as inflammation and being out of place.

The MRI said nothing about it, but the chiropractor had to constantly pop it back in. You could see it on X-ray. I was going to a chiropractor twice a week. Some of the things the chiropractor told me made some sense. He told me to quit drinking coffee and cokes and drink water. He wanted me to start working out. I know a working out will help a strong back. However, none of these specialists really helped me very much.

They really did not listen to what I was telling them. As with most doctors, they are only treating symptoms and not getting to the root cause, and getting rich in the process. I kept telling them just the slightest of activity and my back would be out of place and my head was about to explode. I told my chiropractor I would roll over in bed and my back would jump out of place, and that my neck was constantly popping and felt like I had grit in it.

> **Message from Bob Butts:** This is the very common symptom of dehydration. I had the same problem until I did the Water Cure.

It felt like I was sleeping on a concrete pillow at night. I could never get comfortable. I also told the neurosurgeon this. He said he could bring a dozen 45-year-old men off of the street and none of them would be any worse off than I was. I knew this was not normal. I felt helpless. I tried several other natural remedies - C.O., for one. It did nothing. Then I ordered your Biotype. It did nothing. However, you sent me two packages of sea salt. I thought nothing of it and threw them on the counter. They sat there for three weeks. Then one day I decided to follow your instructions and start taking this with non-chlorinated water. Within four or five days I could tell a noticeable difference.

Not only did it seem like my back was better, but my energy level was out the roof. The headaches started getting less and with less severity. I not only started researching sea salt, but other ailment remedies as well. All of the major ailments - cancer, heart disease, arthritis, diabetes - are tied together in my opinion.

However, when I started taking your sea salt, I read an article on the web about 24 different things sea salt along with water were essential for. Three tipped me off as to what my problem was. One was slobbering all over your pillow at night. Twenty-seven percent of your bones are made of salt, and a salt deficiency is the leading cause of osteoporosis. Also, salt deficiency would lead to irregular heart beats, but would regulate high blood pressure. I had all of these symptoms. I was on the verge of serious health problems. I was severely dehydrated. Luckily, I did not destroy my back during this period because I work extremely hard every day.

I have been taking sea salt for about three months. I am almost completely healed. It is amazing, and so are you. Thank you so much.

My mom had the worst case of arthritis I had ever seen. Neither my mom nor I ever ate much salt, because doctors are constantly telling us it is bad for us.

> **Message from Bob Butts:** Table salt is toxic, but better than no salt. The only thing that should be consumed is unprocessed sea salt.

However, I only wish I could have found you sooner. I watched my mom suffer the last 15 years of her life, and now I know the answer. My mother was a coca cola addict. That may have been my biggest challenge if I could go back in time. I always told her that I thought the cokes were a lot of her problem. But then I had no research to back it up. It was only a guess. I know now she was severely dehydrated. For me, personally, I will never drink soft drinks or coffee again - maybe an occasional cup of decaf. It will only be non-chlorinated water and a pinch of sea salt a couple of times a day.

If I had not received this miracle from you, I would either be insane or dead. The good Lord left us the answers. We have just been brainwashed by big medicine, and all of these man-made products that are killing us - even the water out of our own taps. You and your associates are truly miracles from God. Godly people have integrity. Thank you so much.

Letter sent to Bob Butts from Darrell Stoddard, Founder, Pain Research Institute, - author "Pain Free for Life."

Anonymous
Letter to Jim Bolen, jimbolen@aol.com

I suffered from migraines for the last 11 years. They were so bad that I was recently given Topamax. It seemed to help. However, I weaned myself off of it due to the side effects, and the migraines began to recur. With the Water Cure directions I may have to drink up to as much as three glasses of water at one time, but it halts the pain and I no longer need to take Midrin to get me through.

The list of little things goes on and on: lessening of hyperactivity in the boys, better focus during studies, better sleeping, no more bed-wetting! All of it is a wonderful blessing to our family.

Thank you for putting this out there. It's so simple it makes it hard to believe. My family is a testimony to the fact that it works.

Now, I'd like to ask if you've ever heard about this - helping to restore taste or smell? My grandmother has been considering seeing an ENT for he problem. Drinking one-half glass of water to take her medication once a day was difficult for her. She has been drinking coffee or tea most of her adult life. We now have her drinking up to four 10-ounce glasses of water a day. However, she needs much more than that.

Still, I have noticed that we are having better/longer phone conversations. Her hearing is improving. She rarely asks me to repeat myself now, and it's been just over a week since she began the Water Cure (Half her body weight in ounces of water, adding 1/4 teaspoon of sea salt to her food or on her tongue for every quart of water consumed). She's had difficulty hearing for many years! Do you think the taste and smell will return also?

> **Message from Bob Butts:** Everything is affected by dehydration.

Thank you, Jim, for taking the time to promote this in a way that the average person can grasp. It just makes sense. All of my clients will be hearing about it, and I know they will be blessed as well.

H. Weaver, hweaver@wirefire.com

I found your website from altavista search on the words "cure a migraine headache quick." I was suffering from a severe migraine. I took a darvocet tablet and a Zoloft tablet, prescribed for my headaches. In the past, I was prescribed a multi-drug, which contained barbiturates... can't remember the name.

After reading the web site, I immediately went and got the biggest glass of water I could make up. The headache was gone half way through drinking it... slowly, that is, to avoid the inevitable brain freeze. Anyway, you said email if I would like to talk.

Well, ten years ago in January I was in an auto accident where I received a broken neck and some other spinal damages. Now, to this day, I have back problems... mid-back, shoulder area, muscles, and or course the neck, which caused the migraines.

I have been prescribed almost every drug in the book... some of them in the "n.s.a.i.d." and "s.a.i.d." families, causing me to have bleeding ulcers where I have had twenty-two pints of blood transfused in the period of three years.

I have severe arthritic spurring and suffusion in my neck, disintegrating discs and a lot of pain to the point of pretty much ruining any luster in life, as I once enjoyed before.

Your web site says it is shared as God's gift, and this is wonderful, as I am a devout Christian.

Please tell me more. I'm going now to read on ulcers on your web site and other things as well. I will be saving every bit of text for review later offline, and to share with my family and friends.

I have been hearing a lot about water recently, and in my medical studies over the past ten years have come to a side conclusion that dehydration is a factor in most hospital admittances, but the question is WHY?

> **Message from Bob Butts:** Because it is dehydration that puts most people in hospitals.

Your answer to the diuretic functions of soda drinks and caffeinated beverages was my answer. These cause so many kinds of illnesses, it is difficult to count. I believe that soft drinks are the number one cause of prostate problems in the world today. Perhaps any information on this from your studies would help.

I personally do not have this problem, but much of my family does, as well as bladder problems. I attribute it all to years of soft drinks and coffee.

My main concern is my spine. Any information you share would be a blessing. I'm sure you will be very happy. God bless you all and may your light shine in the public eye very soon. Take care.

> **Message from Bob Butts:** Read our pain testimonials on water-cure2.org. It's very simple.

Mavis Butler, North Queensland, Australia

Dear Dr. Batmanghelidj:

For many years I suffered with headaches. I consulted doctors, neurologists, and chiropractors, and spent hundreds of dollars for head scans and X-rays, all to no avail. At times, only my faith in God kept me from wanting to die, as I lay prone in bed for days on end in pain. No medication would ever stop the pain. It would just seem to run its course and then stop. I could never make any connection between my diet and the headaches, and the only pattern they seemed to follow was to always start a couple of hours after a meal.

> **Message from Bob Butts:** That's because your body was being dehydrated, so you didn't have enough water for digestion. Had you drank 12-16 ounces a half hour before eating, you wouldn't have had any headache.

Then one day a friend told me that he thought my headaches were caused because I never drank enough water. While I knew I didn't actually drink much water, I thought my herbal tea with fruit juices, together with lots of fruits, amply supplied my liquid requirements.

Just three weeks later, I was leafing through a health magazine when an advertisement for your book, *"Your Body's Many Cries for Water,"* just seemed to leap out at my eyes. I bought the magazine and sent for the book. When it came, I eagerly read and re-read it to learn this new concept of water, and as I saw the errors in my drinking habits, I quickly set about to righting them.

Can anyone, without experiencing it for themselves, really understand what it is like to have usually pain-filled days changed to wonderfully painless days, when you can do the things you want to do, instead of being "down with a headache?" Oh, such a blessing for which I thank God continually.

It has taken months to properly hydrate my body, but now a headache is a now-and-again event instead of the norm. I thank a loving and caring God for leading me step-by-step to this wonderful truth. He no doubt tried to lead me a lot earlier, but I was too blind to see.

I thank you, Doctor, for your great work and perseverance in bringing this truth to the people. I lecture to adults at night classes on "Better Food and Eating Habits" and I quickly gave one of my sessions entirely to the body's need for water. I have been able to help many people to better health and much less pain in their lives with this knowledge.

A friend told me he was going into the hospital in a few days' time for stomach and ulcer treatment. I begged him to cancel this and try the water treatment you recommended. He, somewhat reluctantly, did and was amazed and thankful to find his pains stopped, and in time to know that the ulcer had healed, all without medication.

Please let me offer my grateful thanks again and pray that the Lord will bless and guide you and your staff as you work for the better health of humanity.

Headaches: A Final Word

Now you know how to completely avoid headaches. If you get one, a couple of glasses of water and a pinch of sea salt should quickly stop it.

CHAPTER SEVEN: DIABETES

Introduction

> The following letter to the editor by Bob Butts serves as a fitting introduction to this chapter.

The CDC reports diabetes will double by 2050. That will only be true if we become more dehydrated. The truth is that diabetes, according to F. Batmanghelidj, M.D., discoverer of the Water Cure, is simply a state of extreme dehydration, not a disease. It's no more a disease than brown grass is a disease. Prove it to yourself if you have type 2 diabetes. Take a blood sugar reading. Then drink 20 ounces of water, wait twenty minutes, and take another reading. You'll find your blood sugar dropped 20 to 40 points.

From that moment on, if you avoid drinking diuretic drinks like caffeine, alcohol and soda, while drinking water instead, and adding a little sea salt to your diet, your readings will continue to go down to normal - in most cases, in three weeks to two months. Plus, you will notice a lot more healthy changes.

The only reason why diabetes exists is because people are dehydrated, and diabetes is only a symptom of dehydration. More information on the Water Cure at watercure2.org, Youtube, and Facebook.

Testimonials: The following testimonial are from victims of diabetes who have found the "Water Cure., which turns their bodies from acid to alkaline. That restores their immune systems to normal.

Jim Rising - Program & Operations Director, EQ-103.2 & 102.3 -pdjames@hotmail.com

I followed the program on drinking one-half of my body weight in ounces of water daily, along with 1/4 teaspoon unprocessed sea salt per quart of water, exercising, and taking a few supplements daily, and getting plenty of amino acids from eggs, beans, cheeses, butter and nuts. In six months I lost 30 pounds, dropped my glucose from 280 to 130 triglycerides from 698 to 216, A/C from 8.0 to 6.3, and cholesterol from 235 to 156. My doctor reported all was normal.

After starting the Water Cure, I began to feel better almost immediately. After taking a glucose reading and then drinking 20 ounces of water with a pinch of salt on my tongue, it dropped 40 points in 20 minutes.

When you do the Water Cure, your insulin requirements will most likely drop. Be prepared to adjust.

> **Message from Bob Butts:** Listen to Jim explain his amazing recovery on our www.watercur2.org web site. More details in Dr. Batmanghelidj's book, *"Your body's Many Cries for Water,"* pages 123-131, and *"ABC of Asthma, Allergies, and Lupus,"* which covers far more than the name implies and is on his site at www.watercure2.org.

Julie Matayas, 518-793-7185, new5678@roadrunner.com

Julie here. Yes, Bob, you can put my email address and my phone number here. Jim Bolen is helping me with the program. I feel I should mention that he has called me every day, and encouraged me. He has answered every question and relieved every fear that I have had about adding foods that I never thought I could eat, and lower my blood sugar.

I have many other problems. Osteoporosis in both knees is very bad, needing surgery, high blood pressure, very overweight, and severe back pain. All the bad things from a lifetime of NOT drinking water - only milk and soda, then diet soda, coffee, tea, chocolate, and at times alcohol.

But, little by little, things are getting better. It has been only two weeks, and my sugar is coming down so well. Yesterday I was walking in the house like a normal person without all of the stiffness and pain. My back is feeling better. My blood pressure is getting better. I have so much more energy, and feel so much better.

I don't know what to say except "Thank you, again, Jim Bolen, the watercure2.org web site, and people on it, and Dr. B. Thank you all and God bless you."

I would be happy to talk to anyone who would care to respond.

I am from upstate New York. I started the Water Cure program about two weeks ago. I went on it mainly for diabetes. I knew when I was sent back to the doctor that he was going to put me on medication, and I really did not want that. I know that is a lifetime of medication, and only gets more and more.

But I was getting in the 170s and 180s, and once or twice over 200. I tried everything diet-wise, to get it down, where I was not eating carbohydrates at all. And still, no luck. I didn't know what to do. I had Dr. B's book from four years ago and, for some reason, thought of it again. I am grateful that I did. I went on the sites - his and watercure2.org, and learned so much.

I have help with the program, and am taking my water and salt as he prescribes. I also take some orange juice, I eat some bagel, butter, jelly. I eat Hagen daz ice cream if I need the sugar for energy. I eat bake beans, potatoes, fruit, all things to which I would have said "No way can I eat that stuff."

But my sugar readings are now 125, 120, 116, and 112. I am not finished yet. I have a way to go to get my body healthy, but I can see that I am getting there one day at a time. I am so grateful to all that spend so much time, energy, and money to help others. This is changing my life at 69 years of age. This isn't easy to accomplish, but it is happening. I am grateful. Please feel free to contact me.

Humphrey Perez, Trial Consultant, Scranton, PA

A few years ago I suffered a diabetic coma. I was told that I was two stages away from dying. My body was shutting down.

After I recovered from the diabetic coma, I was very lethargic and had a lot of memory loss. I was not able to function at work, and I was also very depressed. A friend of mine then gave me Dr. Batmanghelidj's book, *"Your Body's Many Cries for Water."* I read it several times and was very much impressed.

At that point, I gave up diet sodas and started on the Water Cure. My mind cleared, and I started to remember the work that I was doing, how to do it, and how to function normally again. Water has also controlled my weight, and I am so much happier. When I am under a lot of stress, I respond to water.

I am a trial consultant, and I tell everyone with whom I come in contact about the Water Cure. Doctors do make mistakes.

Kamilah

I am a black 28-year-old, and I have type 2 diabetes. I came across Mr. Bolen and the Water Cure web site, and also a forum. I decided to write to him for the advice that he had offered someone in India. He was very nice and offered me some articles. A week later, I decided to try the Water Cure. I noticed that it didn't cost much for the sea salt and water. Since I didn't have all of the vitamins that he suggested, I decided to just start with the water and sea salt, and IT ACTUALLY WORKED! Mr. Bolen called me about once a week to check on my progress.

After having such a great response, I decided to continue with the program. It is very easy. All you have to do is follow the program, drink the sea salt and water, follow the daily requirements, and exercise. With anything you do in life, you have to be dedicated and willing to follow steps.

John J. Kelly, mymik@yahoo.com

In February, my doctor called me with the results of my blood test and informed me that I had diabetes 2, as my hemoglobin ALC was 7.3 and I weighed 348 pounds. The next day I started the Water Cure, drinking 5-1/2 quarts of water and adding 1-1/4 teaspoons of sea salt to my food. In July, I had another blood test, and my hemoglobin ALC was 5.4, and my weight was down to 296. Also, triglycerides, cholesterol, and glucose readings showed great improvement. I wasn't able to exercise during this time due to a bad back, so these positive results were achieved through water, sea salt, and diet.

I would never have been able to get to this point without the water and sea salt, and am eternally grateful to you and Dr. B. I now tell everyone I know about the Water Cure. Many thanks.

James B. Post, III, LUBECO, Inc., Wilkes-Barre, PA

Approximately eight months ago, I was diagnosed with diabetes. I had read your material on the Water Cure many times, and I am sure, like many others, was very skeptical on how using water with a little sea salt, could help correct serious health problems. I did get advice from my son, who is a doctor in Manhattan, and we agreed to make your Water Cure solution part of my weight loss and blood sugar level induction program.

I have never taken medicine for the diabetes except for watching the foods I eat, using your program, and getting additional exercise.

My blood sugar levels are now normal, and I credit the Water Cure program as the major portion of my success. I strongly recommend that others use your program for general health and well-being.

Please feel free to have anyone call me if they would like to discuss any details involving my success.

Swadesh Dey, India, swadesh3@mail.com
I am having diabetes since last 11 years. First eight years I controlled blood sugar only by dieting. Then started taking tablets and continued for eight months with upward trend of blood sugar. Reading was FBS-220 and PPBS-230. Also I had BP-160/100. After that I started taking insulin, morning - 16, evening - 10 and continued for last two years. I was on medication for BP also.

On 23rd June 2011, I started Water Cure regimen. Total consumption of water 2.5 liters a day, half liter of water each time with sea salt as directed by Dr. B. I got tremendous result in 10 days for BP. It is 116/78 now without medication. My insulin shots also came down and I take five units in the evening and eight units in the morning. Hopefully, I have to stop insulin shots shortly because the way it is progressing.

I have tried lots of regimens in those 11 years. Nothing worked. But Water Cure really works. Thanks, Dr. B. You are GOD to me.

Diabetes: A Final Word

As you can see, Type 2 diabetes is not a disease, no more than brown grass is a disease. Both go away with water. Dr. Batmanghelidj's research has proven that all diabetics are dehydrated. If you have information that supports or contradicts these conclusions, please email Bob Butts at watercure2@comcast.net

I see no reason why 99% of type 2 diabetes victims cannot be cured with the Water Cure.

CHAPTER EIGHT: ADDICTION

Introduction

One dangerous potential complication from chronic drug or alcohol abuse is dehydration - the loss of too much water from the body. Due to the mind-altering effects of chemical dependency, many individuals do not realize that they have reached dangerous levels of dehydration until it is too late.

The addiction-dehydrated body desperately needs the water, but it can refill it successfully only if there is enough salt in the body. When there is not enough salt, the water is removed from the body to keep salt concentration constant.

Dangers of Alcohol-Related Dehydration - Because alcohol is a diuretic, excessive consumption of alcoholic beverages can cause severe dehydration. Furthermore, alcohol strips the body of important vitamins and minerals, like potassium. As a result, an ionic imbalance occurs, leading to the cramps, light-headedness, and thirst commonly associated with dehydration. As the dehydration worsens, the body experiences weakness, fatigue, and thirst pangs - all signs of an urgent need for water.

Because of the numbing of bodily sensations and the inability to act rationally when inebriated, many alcohol-dependent individuals still fail to drink the water their body needs - often interpreting thirst as the need for another alcoholic beverage. If the signs of alcohol-related dehydration continue to be ignored, alcohol-dependent individuals can experience dehydration that requires hospitalization in order to treat. In some cases, alcohol-related dehydration can lead to overheating and death.

Fortunately, many inpatient alcohol recovery centers will ensure that alcohol-dependent individuals receive adequate hydration as part of their physical recovery process. Therefore, it is vital that addicts be made aware that dehydration is the biggest threat to their lives.

The Effects of Dangerous Drug-Related Dehydration - Many drugs can also cause severe dehydration - with many of the main culprits being amphetamines and their derivatives. While active people can lose up to 2.6 liters of water in perspiration, those on drugs such as Meth, Ecstasy and Speed can lose even more as activity levels spike. Additionally, the euphoric and physical sensations associated with amphetamines tend to mask the body's warning signs of hypothermia. This can lead drug-dependent individuals to experience seizures and even die from heat-stroke if they do not receive proper hydration.

Anyone with a drug or alcohol addiction will be amazed at how fast they can get rid of those addictions just by quitting caffeine, soda and alcohol and following the Water Cure. Nothing detoxifies like water and unprocessed sea salt. Doing so will often help cravings to be stifled in a day or two. Not doing so can make quitting nearly impossible. Rehab would improve success rates tremendously if they educated residents to avoid caffeine, alcohol, and soda. It is almost impossible otherwise. Also, maintaining a slightly alkaline pH is critical.

Testimonials: "Forty-five years of alcoholism gone in 24 hours." These testimonials are all from the Natural Healing Center, Wichita, Kansas.

kevinnatural@aol.com

I was a recovering drug addict and alcoholic for 25 years. I was a long-term member of AA, and still suffered from drug and alcohol cravings - anxiety, shakes and general out-of-control feelings. Within 24 hours of starting the Water Cure, all of the symptoms began to subside. My high blood pressure dropped to 110/70. This is the best I have had in years.

Gloria

I was an active alcoholic. Within 24 hours, the alcoholic cravings began to subside. The Water Cure has relieved the compulsive craving for alcohol.

Keith

I was an alcohol and drug user for many years. Hydration relieved withdrawal side effects within 24 hours. I am now using the Water Cure, and I am a strong believer and supporter of this program.

Christy

I am a dry alcoholic. I attended several programs (i.e., anger management and codependent programs, AA) with little or no relief. Within minutes of starting the Water Cure program, I relaxed and felt a calm come over my body like I have never felt in my life. The obsessive and compulsive behavior is going away. Nothing has helped me like the Water Cure.

Don

My father gave me the Water Cure book, and I grasped at what I saw as an unexpected deliverance. I had been an alcoholic since my twenties. I was gratified to discover the power of water to still the cravings of an alcoholic. The extra weight I had put on literally just disappeared. My complexion changed back to a wonderful youthful glow - thanks to Dr. B.'s book, which was decisive in my redemption.

D.E.

My father introduced me to your water discoveries at a very critical time for me and my infant son. I am 35 years old and had been an alcoholic since my twenties. As with most people so afflicted, my personal relationships were rocky and impermanent, and I had a broken marriage behind me. I had also just reached the end of a follow-on relationship, in a fashion that was both shocking and stressful, since I was without resources to continue my life in a city strange to me.

I got into Alcoholics Anonymous determined to prevent any repetition of my agonies. At this point, my father gave me your book and urged me to act on its concept with full resolve. I did so, grasping at what I saw as an unexpected deliverance - like the hand of God. I was gratified to discover the power of water to still the cravings of an alcoholic.

Soon, I realized that alcoholism was really a THIRST SIGNAL that I was habituated to respond to with alcohol, which, is a powerful dehydrating agent. One became like a dog chasing its own tail.

Dehydration through alcohol is self-perpetuating, unless the thirst sensations are answered with water. Persevering with adequate daily water intake, and eliminating dehydrating caffeinated drinks, I found myself able to deal effectively with my personal vocational crisis. I was able to get my belongings and furniture together, rent a truck and load it, and drive myself and my son back to California from Las Vegas. My former alcoholic self could not have done this. I resettled myself in California, went back successfully into my work as a beautician, and buckled down to raising my son.

Of course I still have normal problems like everyone else, but alcohol is not one of them. Water has lifted this curse from my life. As I write, I have been ten months "dry" - but hydrated - and I have been able to reorganize my life rationally.

Adequate daily water intake is the bedrock on which to rebuild a life deranged by alcohol, and to help others do the same. There are other benefits that will have great appeal to all alcoholic women in particular.

As an alcoholic, I had begun to lose my youthful looks. Steady self-poisoning and dehydration with alcohol dulled and aged my complexion. In recent years, my weight had steadily increased for the reasons you outline so clearly in your book. I began to look puffy and pallid. Therefore, I was elated - absolutely "stoked" - when rehydration caused my excess weight to just disappear. I could not believe it, nor could my friends, as I regained the perfect figure I had enjoyed as a young woman. I did not have to "sweat" this. It just happened.

My complexion began to change back to a wonderful youthful glow that everyone remarks on, and which has delighted my father. My regained radiance is a big asset in my professional work as a beautician. The weight loss and adequate daily water intake invigorated my whole being. I began running on what you call "hydro-electric power" in your book.

With these changes came an overall renewal of life and outlook. I continue to help others through AA. I began attracting positive gentlemen of purpose and substance, instead of the lesser fellows who would tolerate an alcoholic woman. Church attendance brought me comfort, and I wanted to attend. I plan and work for an ever-improving life.

Reviewing my past from my normalized perspective, I apologized to my father for my many years of outrages and for the suffering I had caused him because of his love for me. Dad had almost given up on me, but his provision of your book was decisive in my redemption. My father tells everyone that you are one of the greatest physicians in the history of the world. I think he is right.

> **Message from Bob Butts:** I know he is!

Thank you, Dr. Batmanghelidj, for what you have done, not only for me with my turnaround life, but for all mankind.

Just call me **"Freedom at last!"**
Almost every time I got drunk, I would get into a fight. I had no control of myself whatsoever. I ended up in jail too many times. I eventually went on the Water Cure and was amazed that I was able to rid myself of the alcohol cravings that were wrecking my life in just a few days. That was the last time I had any violent behavior. Everything in my life got better, especially relationships....

Michael V. Krol, R.R. #2, Box 1845, Honesdale, PA

Mike_Krol@oneox.com

My life changed two months after the Water Cure. As the result of an accident on October 5, 1954, I suffered a broken back, dislocated shoulder, dislocated knees, a smashed foot, and a fractured skull. I've had severe pain and discomfort ever since. I was taking Lasix, a diuretic for edema of both legs. I also took atenolol and lisinopril for high blood pressure and was told to use no salt.

I was a heavy consumer of alcohol most of my life. It got to where I was drinking one or two six-packs of beer each day, and sometimes as much as a full case. I prayed to God to help me stop drinking.

I first heard about the Water Cure on *"Positive Press on the Air."* My wife and daughter went to Cee-Kay Auto and spoke to Bob Butts about the Water Cure. I sat in the car. It wasn't easy for me to come in.

I read the literature and it made sense to me, so I tried the Water Cure. The day I started drinking a gallon of water a day while using sea salt liberally, I quit drinking alcohol. I've had no desire for any since, even when in the company of others drinking alcohol. My pain is diminished to the point that I don't park in handicap spots. I am now off of all pain medication.

The edema in my ankles disappeared in two days. In two weeks my blood pressure returned to normal and I've been off the medication since. Before going on medication my pressure was 166 over 126. On medication it would be about 156 over 83. Now it is 141 over 78. My energy also greatly improved. It's incredible how much my life changed for the better in just two months.

I recommended the Water Cure to my daughter Kelly, who was suffering from compacted bowels. In five days she was restored to health. Her complexion also greatly improved. She had very severe blemishes and skin texture that was so bad it resembled alligator hide. It returned to almost normal in five days. She now feels like a million dollars.

Feel free to share my success with your listeners and readers. You may use my name, address and telephone number.

Addiction: A Final Word

There you have the proof. The reason it has been so difficult to get rid of addiction is because the dehydration made it impossible. Now, if only we can get rid of our addiction to money and power.

CHAPTER NINE: BACK PAIN

Introduction

Back pain is known as one of humanity's most frequent complaints. It is also the number one cost of insurance claims. In the U.S., acute low back pain (also called lumbago) is the fifth most common back pain. About nine out of ten adults experience back pain at some point in their lives, and five out of ten working adults have back pain every year.

The spine is a complex interconnecting network of nerves, joints, muscles, tendons, and ligaments, and all are capable of producing pain, especially in a dehydrated body. Large nerves that originate in the spine and go to the legs and arms can make pain radiate to the extremities.

Unfortunately, science has not realized that almost all back problems are simply the result of dehydration, which causes the cartilage and the discs to degenerate. Correct the dehydration and the cartilage will regenerate in most cases.

The following testimonials will prove that dehydration is the main cause of all back problems.

Testimonials: The following testimonials are from victims of back pain who have found the "Water Cure."

Alan G. Burley - Letter sent to Darrell Stoddard

I want to personally thank you for saving my life. There are very few good doctors with any integrity left. It is all about the money. I forgot if I got your web site from Kevin Trudeau's book, or Bottom Line Health. It does not really matter. It is only important that I found you.

Two years ago, it seemed as though it happened overnight, but my symptoms were gradually becoming more noticeable over time. Starting in my teens, I thought it was just old age creeping up on me.

First, it started with knee injuries, then my upper back and neck started really bothering me at 41 years of age. I had been in a car wreck five or six years prior to these symptoms. I thought it was the result of the wreck, but sometimes this does not show up for several years. The headaches were miserable, always in my neck, back of the head, an top of the head. It seemed like I went for a solid year and had a headache every day.

I went to orthopedic, chiropractor, neurosurgeon, and general doctor. I had an MRI done that said I had a mild bulging disk in my neck C6, slight herniating of T3 and T4, and a mild herniating at T8, tn. T3 and T4 were off the machine. T6 was the worst of all as far as inflammation and being out of place. The MRI said nothing about it, but the chiropractor had to constantly pop it back in. You could see it on X-ray. I was going to a chiropractor twice a week.

Some of the things the chiropractor told me made some sense. He told me to quit drinking coffee and cokes, and drink water. He wanted me to start working out, which I know a strong back does help. However, none of these specialists really helped me very much. They really did not listen to what I was telling them, as with most doctors. They are only treating symptoms and not getting to the root cause, and getting rich in the process. I kept telling the doctors just the slightest activity and my back would be out of place, and my head was about to explode. I told my chiropractor I would roll over in bed and jump out of place, and that my neck was constantly popping and felt like I had grit in it.

Message from Bob Butts: This is a very common symptom of dehydration. I had a bad back myself before I learned about the Water Cure.'

It felt like I was sleeping on a concrete pillow at night. I could never get comfortable. I also told the neurosurgeon this, and he said he could bring a dozen 45-year-old men off of the street, and not one of them would be any worse off than I was. I knew this was not normal. I felt helpless. I tried several other natural remedies, C.O. for one, and it did nothing. However, you sent me two packages of sea salt. I thought nothing of it and threw them on the counter. They sat there for three weeks.

Then one day I decided to follow your instructions and started taking this with non-chlorinated water. Within four to five days, I could tell a noticeable difference. Not only did it seem like my back was better, but my energy level was off the roof, and the headaches started getting less and with less severity. I not only started researching sea salt, but other aliment remedies. All of the major ailments - cancer, heart disease, arthritis and diabetes - are tied together in my opinion.

However, when I started taking your sea salt, I read an article on the web about 24 different things sea salt, along with water, were essential for. Three tipped me off as to what my problem was. One was slobbering all over your pillow at night; 27% of your bones are made of salt, and a salt deficiency was the leading cause of osteoporosis, and salt deficiency would lead to irregular heart beats, but the proper amount would regulate high blood pressure. I had all of these symptoms. I was on the verge of serious health problems. I was severely dehydrated. Luckily, I did not destroy my back during this period, because I work extremely hard every day.

I have been taking sea salt for about three months. I am almost completely healed. It is amazing, and so are you. Thank you so much.

My mom had the worst case of arthritis I had ever seen before she passed away. Neither my mom nor I ever ate much salt, because the doctors are constantly telling us it is bad for us, and it may be. However, I only wish I could have found you sooner. I watched her suffer the last 15 years of her life, and now I know the answer. My mother was a coca cola addict. That may have been my biggest challenge if I could go back in time. I always told her I thought the cokes were a lot of her problem. Then, I had no research to back it up. It was only a guess. I know now she was severely dehydrated.

For me, personally, I will never drink soft drinks or coffee again - maybe an occasional cup of decaf. It will only be non-chlorinated water and a pinch of sea salt a couple of times a day. If I had not received this miracle from you, I would either be insane or dead. The good Lord left us the answers. We have just been brainwashed by big medicine, and all of these man-made products that are killing us - even the water out of our own taps. You and your associates are truly miracles from God. Godly people have integrity. Thank you so much.

Todd Vogt

Dear Bob Butts:

I have been experiencing back pain for about 20 years. Each year it got worse and worse. Two years ago it got so bad that I was going to have to go on state disability. I have been a hard-working construction worker for years, and the thought of being unable to work was sending me into depression.

About one year ago, my friend told me about the Water Cure for my asthma. Several days after starting the Water Cure, I noticed my back pain was gone. This was amazing!! I didn't realize that it was from the water until I went a day without drinking much water. I had a bad back incident. I couldn't even go to church the next day, so I started drinking the salt water, and by lunch time my pain was gone.

I want to thank you, Bob, for opening my eyes to the fact that God put the cure for my problems all around me. I have never been this healthy. I don't get sick anymore, either.

God bless you.

Fran Slavetski

I believe Bob Butts is one of the greatest men in this area. He is not only a successful businessman in the area, but he is a great humanitarian.

"I have tried the Water Cure and feel so much better. I drink more than 64 ounces of water and have given up caffeine."

I previously had severe back pain and had trouble bending and lifting. I have noticed I feel so much better. I prefer water to any other liquid and have not been sick or missed work for seven years, and work seven days a week, 18 hours per day. I am 49 years old.

I am appreciative of Bob Butts for turning me on to water.

Message from Bob Butts: All I did was to pass on to you what I learned from Dr. B. Thanks for your hard work. I'm sure you will also help many people.

Dorman J. Bryce

Dear Dr. Batmanghelidj:

On June 29, 1995, I hurt my back. On June 30, 1995, in a lot of pain, I called my medical doctor. He was closed and I couldn't see him until July 3. On June 30, I went to the chiropractor. He took X-rays, gave treatment, and I received some relief. July 3, I saw my medical doctor. He examined me and then sent me to a physical therapist for three different days. I had some relief, but not much.

I returned to my medical doctor on July 10, still in pain. He gave me some pain pills and took an X-ray and CAT-Scan of my lower spine. He also sent me back to the physical therapist for three more days. Again, some relief.

On July 13, still in pain, my medical doctor sent me to have an MRI on my back. Also, during this time, I had two more chiropractor visits. During all the above time, I was on pain pills twice a day.

My wife remembered reading in Dr. Julian Whitaker's *Health and Healing Letters* (March 95, Vol. 5, No. 3) where he mentioned your book, *"How to Deal with Back Pain and Rheumatoid Joint Pain."*

My wife went to a local book store and purchased the book for $14.95. We hurriedly read your book, did the exercises you suggested, and started drinking water. WITHIN ONE HOUR MY BACK WAS PAIN FREE, and has remained ever since. God bless you.

What really ticks me off is:

- Medical doctor charged for 3 visits $150.00
- Physical Therapist charged for 3 visits   661.50
- X-rays and CAT-Scan   209.00
- Chiropractor @-rays, 3 visits   155.00
- MRI   543.50
- Santaiam Memorial Hospital   129.00

TOTAL CHARGES (with very little relief) $1,838.00

Your book and instruction only cost $14.95, and you gave me almost immediate relief in only one treatment!!

Again, God bless you for your books and knowledge. We ow also have your book, *"Your Body's Many Cries for Water,"* your video and your tape. They are all exceptional. If you publish anything else, I want them.

> **Message from Bob Butts:** Strange. Science keeps charging more for less, while the Water Cure charges nothing and keeps giving more

Harry Finn

My wife, Carol, and I will be forever grateful for showing us the most simple, economical way to better health. To think, all you have to do is drink eight glasses of water and one quarter teaspoon of sea salt per quart per day. I now know that anyone who does this will see a considerable improvement in their health. I have yet to hear anyone who has taken that advice say they haven't noticed a difference. It works. You just have to do it. No one can do it for you.

So, people who are looking for better health through water must be made aware of the variables. For every cup of coffee I drink, I also drink an added glass of water. For every glass of soda, I do the same. Afer a short time, you lose the taste for these other drinks.

I remember the first time I drank diet soda. I hated the taste because that's all my family used to buy. I started to acquire a taste for it. Then, I hated the taste of regular soda. The same holds true when you start to drink water on a regular basis. Now I can't stand the taste of any soda. I never would have thought the day would come when I would enjoy a tall glass of cold FILTERED water with a pizza pie. That's right! I can't even drink soda with pizza. Water tastes much better.

I still enjoy two cups of coffee in the morning, but I drink a glass of water before each cup.

Some of the benefits we've reaped from taking your advice are: 99% less back pain, a higher energy level, the absence of severe migraine headaches, and, finally, a thirst that needs quenching. For the past 20 years, I never drank because I was thirsty. I drank because I believe drinking diet soda becomes habitual. Since I started drinking water, I found that I drink because I'm actually thirsty. That alone amazes me.

I was diagnosed as having a herniated disc. I will never ever forget the pain that used to shoot down my legs if I moved the wrong way. There were times my wife had to put my socks on me in the morning. Then I would have to crawl out of bed. I couldn't sit in a chair, any kind of chair, for six months. If I was standing when the pain hit, it would knock me right to the ground, where I would stay until I could muster up the courage to crawl to the couch or bed. Sometimes I would just lie where I was for hours.

To get to the doctors, I had to lie on my stomach in the car. I had to eat at the kitchen table standing up. Now, don't get me wrong. The doctor helped me. The pills I took for inflammation and the pills I took for pain helped. All the time I couldn't have endured without them.

Here's what I'm saying. The first year I had a prescription for the original bottle and three refills, all of which were used in one year. The second year I started drinking the water and I used only one bottle of pills in one year. I really think I could have done without those pills the second year, but the pain was so horrendous, it seemed as if I needed that little bit of extra insurance once in a while if I felt the slightest twinge in my buttocks. (That's where the pain would always originate.)

I'm convinced that the pills eased the pain at the time, but the water aided in the cure. The reason I say aided is because I also had to start walking and exercising. When I saw the big improvement in my health, I almost naturally started eating more of the right foods. It seems as if everything starts falling into place once you make it a way of life. I'm not a health purist. I still smoke. But, you know what? I smoke less. I still don't live or breathe or eat every hour of the day in the way that's best, but, overall, I'm in much better health now than I was a couple of years ago.

For the most part, everything in moderation never killed anyone. I even started bowling a couple of months ago. At one time I was convinced that I would never be able to pick up a 16-pound bowling ball and throw it down an alley. I owe this new way of life to you, Bob Butts. Thank you.

I'm writing this letter in the hope other people will see it , and maybe it will motivate them just enough to try it. If I help just one good person, it will have been worth it.

I am forever indebted to you.

> **Message from Bob Butts:** His dog story is on CD #4 (see resources in back matter.)

Lloyd Palmer

I read Dr. Batman's book about 10 months ago. I found his claims astonishing and intriguing. When I read his explanation of the hydraulics of the spinal column, and how dehydration compresses the disks, causing back pain, I decided to try his remedy, because I suffer from ankylosis spondylitis (a form of rheumatoi arthritis), and from mild hypertension.

Believe me, it was not easy to drink the required amount of water each day, simply because I had not been a big water drinker. I forced myself to do it, and was rewarded for my effort. I have had no severe flare-ups on my spinal column since I began the water regimen. You had to have been in my shoes to appreciate what this means to me. Being laid up with spinal vertebrae inflammation many times each year, and as a result resembling "a walking comma," is very debilitating and painful. My elevated blood pressure has also returned to normal.

I consider Dr. Batman's information as God-sent. It is my prayer that you, too, will benefit from his pain-relieving and life-extension revelations. Adults should drink at least eight eight-ounce glasses of water per day to hydrate their bodies.

Dr. Batman also reminds us to make sure that you have at least 1/4 teaspoon of sea salt on your food for every auart of water you drink to help your body utilize the added water intake. The sea salt is crucial. Always drink water between meals, and not with meals. Dr. Batman recommends that you drink at least a half-hour before meals and about two-and-a-half hours after meals for best results. This time schedule for water intake will help digestion rather than dilute it.

Also, don't think for a moment that drinking coffee, soda pop, diet colas, tea, or fruit drinks is a substitute for water. When Dr. Batman prescribes eight eight-ounce glasses of water, he means just that. Most coffee, pop and tea are dehydrating drinks. In other words, they're diuretic. Their liquid isn't available to irrigate your system because of the caffeine and/or phosphates they contain.

If you can't give up these dehydrating liquids, just make certain you don't count their intake as part of your eight eight-ounce glasses of water each day.

> **Message from Bob Butts:** By the way, Paul Harvey told Lloyd Palmer's story on his daily radio show.

Tom Johnson

Please accept the following statement as a testimonial to the Water Cure.

I started the Water Cure to relieve nagging lower back pain. Not only did it cure that, it cured bursitis that I had in my shoulder, eliminated my need to take antacids for my stomach, and antihistamines I was taking for chronic allergies and, if that weren't enough, I no longer have dandruff. I could add that it lowered my cholesterol and blood pressure, but someone might think I am stretching the truth. I'm not! Thank you.

> **Message from Bob Butts:** At this time, Tom Johnson was Sales Manager for Nickson Industries, a well-known exhaust parts supplier for the automotive industry. Sadly, no matter how many great recoveries are seen, the automotive industry is completely ignorant to the benefits of the Water Cure (but it whines about health costs).

Work Kebede, 2904 Stonybrook Drive, Bowie, MD 20715 301-332-0245

My name is Work A. Kebede. I am an Ethiopian-American and a former journalist from *"Voice of America,"* Washington, D.C. After I retired in 2005, I stumbled onto Dr. Batmanghelidij's book, *"Water for Health, for Healing, for Life."* I couldn't believe that drinking plain water could really cure illness.

In 2006, I enthusiastically started to follow the program. For a few months, I did it successfully and saw some positive results. But then I stopped drinking water as I should. Instead, I started drinking wine, beer and some other strong alcoholic drinks, and I forgot about watching my diet. I also ignored reading the book, which I bought several copies of at first for friends and relatives. As a result, I got back all of those pains which I had started to get rid of.

I saw my body weight going up and my lower back pain getting worse. My legs couldn't carry my weight, and I could hardly walk a quarter of a mile without taking a rest. My blood pressure was up, I had arthritis pain, and whenever I had a glass of wine, I was suffering from heartburn, which was only relieved with anti-acid medicine.

Then I decided to lose my weight by picking up the Water Cure book. On May 2, 2010, I started the program. The program worked wonders for my health. I started walking early in the morning and late in the evening. I increased my intake of water. I watched my diet, cut down on the coffee, and practically eliminated alcohol drinks. Gradually, I saw improvements. After almost four months, I have lost 26 pounds, my lower back pain is gone, sciatica done with, arthritis disappeared, blood pressure excellent, energy up, walking increased to four miles a day. And, that is the result I saw after drinking more and more water daily, with a pinch of sea salt here and there.

Mr. Butts, while I am seeing such a great improvement in my personal life, I couldn't help thinking about the poor people of my native country, Ethiopia. As you may know, Ethiopia is one of the poorest countries in the world. The average people live on a dollar a day, life span for the average person is 50 years, and there is a huge shortage of doctors and medical facilities. Those who are there do not have enough time for the average person to visit them.

I realized that, if the people of Ethiopia had the information of the Water Cure, and increased their water intake daily, a lot of lives could be saved, and the country could have a more productive society.

I would love to start a campaign in Ethiopia to inform the people about the advantage of drinking water for better health and longer life.

I pray to the Almighty that my prayers will one day be fulfilled. Thank you and God bless you.

Back Pain: A Final Word

Get your life <u>back</u> and keep it pain-free. Do the Water Cure and tell the world. The Water Cure is Dr. Batmanghelidj's great gift to humanity in a world full of physical and economic pain. The Water Cure represents the good that can happen when people from around the world come together, spreading the truth of the Water Cure. If only government would do the same thing.

CHAPTER TEN: OBESITY

Introduction

> A letter to the editor from Bob Butts to the Citizens Voice (Scranton, PA), and an article in New York papers jointly serve as the introduction to this chapter.

"Dehydration causes obesity: Water Cure can break cycle"
One of the worst problems in the U.S. is obesity, and solving it is not even a challenge. One just needs to follow Dr. Batmanghelidj's free Water Cure.

Of course, our mentality is to believe that if it is free, then it is too good to be true, so it can't be. Maybe the only way to get everyone to try it is to charge people for every pound they lose, and then people will love it, because they will be paying for results only. All people do now is continue to pay a ton of money for high-profit non-solutions to obesity that have extremely low success rates.

The only real cure for obesity is to correct the cause, and the cause is extreme dehydration, lack of water, salt and electrolytes due to over use of soda, caffeine or alcohol. Bet you can't find one single obese person who isn't dehydrated.

The reason dehydration makes a person obese is when a person isn't getting enough water, the brain will make you crave food to get the water from the food.

When you quit the caffeine and alcohol, and consume enough water and salt, your brain has no reason to keep you craving food so your weight falls off.

If you want the water and salt the medical way, just get saline IVs at $599 each, or Google ORT (Oral Rehydration Therapy) and learn why India and Bangladesh call this the "magic bullet." It is made up of water, salt and sugar. Professional athletes have long been taking saline IVs as a performance enhancer, which led to the development of Gatorade.

Remember, if it is from God it is free, has no side effects, and it works. That describes the Water Cure.

–Bob Butts

Drink till you drop. A magic elixir is shown to promote weight loss - New York, August 24th**, 2010 -** "Consume more water and you will become much healthier" goes an old wives' tale. "Drink a glass of water before meals and you will eat less" goes another. Such prescriptions seem sensible, but they have little rigorous science to back them up.

Until now, that is... A team led by Brenda Davy of Virginia Tech has run the first randomized, controlled trial studying the link between water consumption and weight loss. A report on the 12-week trial, published earlier this year, suggested that drinking water before meals does lead to weight loss. At a meeting of the American Chemical Society in Boston this week, Dr. Davy unveiled the results of a year-long follow-up study that confirms and expands that finding.

The researchers divided 48 inactive Americans, aged 56 to 75, into two groups. Members of one were told to drink half a liter of water (a bit more than an American pint) shortly before each of three daily meals. The others were given no instructions on what to drink.

Before the trial, all participants had been consuming between 1,800 and 2,200 calories a day. When it began, the women's daily rations were slashed to 1,200 calories, while the men were allowed 1,500. After three months, the group that drank water before meals had lost about 7kg (15-1/2 pounds) each, while those in the thirsty group lost only 5kg.

Dr. Davy confidently bats away some obvious doubts about the results. There is no selection bias, she observes, since this is a randomized trial. It is possible that the water displaced sugary drinks in the hydrated group, but this does not explain the weight loss, because the calories associated with any fizzy drinks consumed by the other group had to fall within the daily limits.

Moreover, the effect seems to be long-lasting. In the subsequent 12 months, the participants have been allowed to eat and drink what they like. Those told to drink water during the trial have, however, stuck with the habit - apparently they like it. Strikingly, they have continued to lose weight (around 700g over the year),, whereas the others have put it back on.

Why this works is obscure. But work it does. It's cheap, and it's simple. And unlike so much dietary advice, it seems to be enjoyable, too.

> **Message from Bob Butts:** It is not obscure. Just read the following testimonials. Now, if only we can get the world to listen.

Testimonials: The following testimonials are from victims of obesity who have found the "Water Cure."

Anonymous

An update for you. After one year plus, I have lost almost 60 pounds. It's to the point where my friends and family think I am too skinny, but I feel great! I now weigh about 168 and am able to run nearly three to four miles a day, sometimes up to six. I could never run before as my knees and legs always hurt. Drinking water has helped me to live a healthier life, that's for sure! I plan to keep drinking H_2O and keep up the sea salt as well.

I used to drink coffee all day long and pop two to three cans a day. I now drink only two cups of coffee in the morning and have an occasional pop as a treat before supper.

I seemed to hit plateaus in weight loss, and then lose 10-12 pounds at a shot. However, I do not care to lose much more weight, so I am going to try to make sure that I eat enough complex carbohydrates to maintain a steady weight of 165 pounds with my exercise plan. Thanks.

> **Message from Bob Butts:** Two cups of coffee is still too much.

Steve Kreger, Danville, PA, kruegman1@aol.com

"Water Cure washes away 130 pounds, free of all symptoms of diabetes - without dieting and at no cost." The whole thing was a "breeze." The 310-pound Steve Kreger of Danville heard from a friend about how easy it was to lose weight by following the Water Cure. He decided he also would give it a try, thinking to himself, "What do I have to lose other than a lot of weight?" He had little or no energy and was a diabetic.

Soon after starting the Water Cure, Steve found himself feeling great, with unexplained energy. He can now play with his five children and his whole life changed for the better. Within four months he lost eighty pounds, and in a little over a year he lost another fifty pounds, for a grand total of 130 pounds. He did all this without going on a diet.

With his newfound energy, he is very active and has easily maintained his weight at 180 pounds without effort for about three years. Once he got rid of his addiction to Diet Mountain Dew, everything else was easy.

It took Steve 4-5 months till his blood/sugar readings normalized. He is now free of all symptoms of diabetes and takes no medication. *Conclusion:* "I tried many diets and nothing worked, but the free Water Cure totally changed my life."

Roger M. Weeden, Tasmania, rojan@southcom.com.au
First, thanks for the tapes and reading material. Well, we have been on the water/salt for three months now. Yes, there have been changes, subtle at first, but now evident. For example, Janet and I lost three and four kgs respectively. Janet now has her dimples in her cheeks again. They have not been evident for several years. We are both feeling lighter and more alive inside ourselves. We are coping with some added pressures a lot better than we would normally have done. Janet is now walking every second day for about three kms, without feeling knocked out.

We shared this concept of water and salt with one of our daughters. She stopped the tablets and has been on water for seven days. No soreness, a feeling of life has returned. She has passed the message on to another of our daughters, and we will see what will happen.

Thanks to the good doctor. Thanks to yourself for taking the message to the people. Stay happy and keep up the great work.

David Rogers, Video5@Superaje.com

I have joined the Water Cure "crusade" spreading the word. I have done a write-up at my Gourmet Garden site and added the link to our site, and I've sent the link out to my mailing list. I guess I should have asked permission first, but somehow have the feeling you would approve. There's no marketing at my site either.

After about ten days of the water and salt, I feel fantastic. I also quit sugar and coffee, and it really helps. I am losing my big belly so rapidly that my pants are falling off of me. Thank you for sharing and caring.

Richard T. Healy, Executive Director: Automotive Wholesale Association of New England

Our E.A.P. specialist has been on the water program for about seven weeks. He weighed in at 295. He has presently lost 40 pounds. He has lost all traces of diabetes. His asthma has been noticeably relieved, and his skin has improved. He now plays golf without back pain and, incidentally, this is very important to him.

He is the biggest enthusiast we have and, as you know, as an E.A.P. Specialist, he is in the field contacting the people covered by our insurance trust daily, in that his specialty is drug addiction and alcoholism. He has taken many of our tapes, quite a few of our books, and is promoting the program personally.

I've been on the program for quite a while, and I feel that my indigestion has improved, my taste far more precise, and overall I feel it's working. The same situation holds true for Phil Grisafi, our insurance Manager. He is a young guy in his thirties, and to my knowledge, he's very, very pleased with the results of the Water cure so far.

Will keep you posted. Once again, thank you for all of your efforts and dedication.

Mark Chilek, Moosic, PA

For most of my life, I had been overweight. Every family has a "fat child" and this was me. I was told I was just "big-boned" and I should be content with who I was. Then I heard about the Water Cure.

I was skeptical at first, but thought that all I really had to lose was my weight. Over the period of a year and a half, I lost approximately 100 pounds, and I am no longer the "fat kid" that everyone knew.

But, besides losing weight, I have noticed that my acid reflux, which had been a MAJOR part of my life, had now gone. I could now enjoy foods that previously had brought me nothing but sickness.

I have also noticed that I no longer get ear infections, which also seemed commonplace to me at one time.

So, not only did I lose almost 100 pounds, but also acid reflux and ear infections, both of which seem inevitable problems of life. Also, I have more energy and feel as if I have become a whole new person. I have the energy to do the things which would easily have worn me out previously.

Obesity: A Final Word

It is much easier to lose 50 or more pounds than 10 or 20. That's because, when a person doesn't drink much water, and/or drinks caffeinated or alcoholic drinks that take water out of the body creating a greater water shortage, the body will create hunger in order to get the water from the food. The result is tremendous weight gain. Jut as soon as that person starts drinking a lot of water, the hunger cravings start to subside. Therefore, it is easy to lose weight when you aren't hungry and the pounds fall of, and you don't need a diet. With your new-found energy, you'll find it easy to do the best exercise, walking. Send us your stories. If you just need help, just email us at watercure2@comcast.net

This question/answer format is a fitting conclusion for this chapter on obesity.

Fine Tuning for Maximum Weight Loss

Question: Why do we need to replace fluids lost from the body by drinking plenty of water?

Answer: Our bodies are mostly made up of water - 75%. This water needs to be replaced daily because:

- Approximately three pints of water per day are lost through the kidneys.

- Approximately one pint of water per day is lost through the skin in perspiration.

- A further pint is lost through breathing and vaporization.

Question: What happens if we do not replace this lost water in our bodies on a daily basis?

Answer: The body will seek out the replacement water it needs from the water in our organs, blood, and undigested sludge sitting in the intestines, waiting to be eliminated.

Question: What effect will that have on the body?

Answer: As water is withdrawn from this sludge, the fecal matter becomes harder, resulting in constipation. The body will retain water to dilute these toxic substances, and bloating and weight gain will occur. Because the water from the undigested sludge is dirty, when it is re-circulated throughout the body, it will increase the toxins in the body. This can lead to feelings of tiredness and lethargy, and the body will be more vulnerable to infection.

Question: How many glasses of water should e drink every day?

Answer: Half your body weight in ounces.

Question: How can we increase our daily intake?

Answer: Plenty of exercise. Walk one half hour in AM and PM. Drink two glasses of water first thing in the morning and last thing at night, as a reminder. Carry water in your car, and keep a glass at your desk. Replace soft drinks and cordials with plain, room-temperature water. Aim to increase your daily intake slowly over time, and be prepared to urinate more frequently, as your body flushes out toxins.

Question: What are the benefits?

Answer: You will experience greater feelings of well-being, fewer illnesses, an increase in your energy level, fewer weight problems, and a healthy digestive system that is free of constipation.

> **Message from Bob Butts:** Also see *"Woman's World"* article in the Media Section in the front matter of this book, or Google *Womans World: The slimming new water cure. The testimonials will amaze you.*

CHAPTER ELEVEN: AMPUTATION

Introduction

This chapter discusses amputations and how to avoid them. According to Dr. Batmanghelidj, almost all amputation are done as a result of poor circulation can be avoided. Read Drew Bauman's story below on how, after being told he would need to have both legs amputated, he started drinking water. His legs greatly improved because his circulation returned.

In summertime, when the grass turns brown because it doesn't have enough moisture, therefore depriving the blades of circulation, would you think the grass should be amputated? Of course not, because that would be crazy. And in most cases it is absolutely insane to cut off a person's toes, feet, and legs when their lack of circulation is simply due to lack of water.

I think it is absolutely impossible to have diabetic neuropathy in the limb of a person who is well-hydrated. Medical schooling has not made doctors aware of this.

If you are facing amputation, and if your doctor thinks that you can put if off safely, try the Water Cure for a week. I'm sure you will be astonished.

Testimonials: The following testimonials are from victims facing amputation who have found the Water Cure.

Andrew J. Bauman, IV, Scranton, PA

This is my testimony about my pain that I used to suffer from, and how I avoided amputation of my legs.

I am Andrew J. Bauman, IV, and I have had diabetic neuropathy (diabetic since April 1971 at age 14).

Even the diabetic neuropathy, which is "still there" and measurable by nerve conduction tests (I show zero electrical responses), gives me no more pain and is much better (NO MORE PAIN). I continue to improve.

My ankles and legs no longer swell as they used to, and the promise/warning that they would have to "cut off my legs" due to veins bursting (venous insufficiency) when they injected dye to test for the extent of damage, is no longer there. I have normal size ankles/legs and I walk now, and the skin color constantly gets lighter.

I still have my legs 25 years later after they told me I would lose them within a year or so! Thanks, Bob Butts for introducing me to the Water Cure, and Dr. B.

Radio Announcement - **September 2010 - by Bob Butts**
An acquaintance told me his wife had a leg amputated because of bad circulation, and the other may need to be done. I said, "That's crazy." According to F. Batmanghelidj, Water Cure discoverer, not drinking enough water or drinking diuretic drinks - caffeine, alcohol or soda - are the main causes of dehydration and bad circulation. Because blood is 94% water, and those drinks deplete the water, and his wife drank a lot of soda, it's no wonder she had bad circulation. Medical schools don't teach this and doctors are erroneously taught to call obvious symptoms of dehydration incurable diseases.

Testimonials from doctors explain this in Dr. B's book. *"Rx for a Healthier Pain Free Life."* It can be borrowed at Cee-Kay Auto. It would be easier for teenagers to understand this, because they aren't being threatened with loss of jobs or licenses if they don't keep the truth of the Water Cure quiet, nor do they have any medical training to prejudice their thinking, or have drug salesmen calling on them and offering them rewards for pushing drugs on patients.

So why do you think the news media, legislators or anyone that makes money on pain and suffering won't talk to me about the Water Cure's success? Maybe because it's free and works? Why not ask them? More information at watercure2.org.

Amputation: A Final Word
I can't tell you how many obviously dehydrated people had their legs needlessly cut off. When grass turns brown, you

don't amputate the brown portion, because it will turn green once it is watered.

The same will happen to black, dehydrated legs once that person drinks water, takes some unprocessed sea salt, and quits caffeine, alcohol and soda.

Go to our interview with Marie Schambrady, M.D. of Alexandria, Virginia, and listen to her tell how she prevented the leg amputation on Youtube and Facebook under "Water Cure" (*The information is also in watercure2.org.*)

–Bob Butts.

CHAPTER TWELVE: EDEMA

Introduction

Edema is swelling caused by the buildup of abnormal amounts of fluid in the body. It is also called "fluid retention" and is often referred to as "dropsy." Fluid collects in specific parts of the body, including legs, arms, feet, and/or hands. According to *Medical News Today*, approximately 4.4 million people in the USA have edema. Diuretics are a popular - but wrong and often deadly - treatment for edema, as this book will demonstrate.

> **Message from Bob Butts:** We suggest you also read Dr. Batmanghelidj's *"Your Body's Many Cries for Water"* for more information.

Testimonials: The following testimonials are from victims of edema who have found the "Water Cure."

Helen J. Morin, idophotography@townisp.com
One morning at 3:00 there was a radio program that changed my life. I was working on a video project when I heard a doc-

tor discussing the Water Cure on the *Art Bell show*. I listened with much skepticism, but when he started talking about the amount of water our body is made up of, it piqued my interest. I conveyed this tale to a very close friend and learned that he also heard it and bought some sea salt. My friend told me about his brother, who is quite sickly. His brother has been feeling better, and the only thing he was doing differently was drinking water and using sea salt.

I started using the sea salt. I have had severe swelling of my ankles ever since going on a certain medication. They would be two- to two-and-a-half inches thick by mid-morning, and that hurt like heck. Walking was becoming a chore for me. I am only in my early fifties, and far too young for this to happen.

I am a wedding and video photographer. This problem has been interfering with the number of events I could book in a year. It is very tough to be on your feet for an eight- to ten-hour day of work with feet that are extremely painful. I would bring three changes of shoes, hoping that this would ease the pain. All three pairs were of the comfortable - not for appearances - variety. This did not help at all, and sometimes I was unable to put a pair back on because of the swelling.

Within the first two days of using the Water Cure, my ankles were normal, and I could see the bones again!!! I was in disbelief. This is something I had not expected. You know how you equate water and increased swelling. Well, the sea salt had worked for me.

I recently went on a business trip to Oklahoma City and had not brought any sea salt. Within 12 hours my ankles were as swollen as ever and hurting like heck. As soon as I got home, I drank two glasses of salt water and, by morning, the swelling was going down. It has been a blessing and a miracle for me. I am so glad I was up at three AM that day. God works in strange ways.

I recommended the Water Cure to a nurse a month ago. I just saw her yesterday. She is THRILLED! She no longer has swollen ankles or aching legs and feet.

Thank you for such a simple and inexpensive cure for my problem.

> **Message from Bob Butts:** I was on that show four hours with Dr. B. The results were phenomenal. The show is repeated, but we were never allowed on "Coast to Coast" again. We were also told we could not rebroadcast that interview. Please contact "Coast to Coast" and ask why.

Fermin A. Romero, Jr.

I suffered from childhood nephrosis for more than ten years (adrenal hormones signal kidneys to retain salt and spill protein in urine; edema).

As an adult, I suffered from allergies. I started drinking large amounts (one to two gallons) of water daily about 30 years ago. This helped. But, I still suffered from allergies and occasional bouts of edema during long gray winters when outside activity was limited. Cold hands and feet, dull aches and pains were common; mental acuity was slow. Summers were different. I felt energetic and mentally clear. My summer diet included more salt. Years of searching modern medical and alternative health information left me puzzled.

Then I discovered your work. I increased my salt intake to recommended levels, and it all went away. Most significant: improved mental clarity, edema gone, dull muscle aches gone, hands and feet now warm, no allergies or nasal congestion, increased energy, balanced urination throughout the day. I sleep better. It is easier to fall asleep. I awake more refreshed. Sugar cravings are a thing of the past. Nervous energy transformed into productive energy. Memory improved. Athlete's foot gone. (Body pH more alkaline.)

I'm lucky that the prednisone and salt-free diet as a child didn't kill me. I get healthier every year, and many cannot believe my age.

Thanks for revealing such simple, wonderful information. I see your work as a part of the "Christ Consciousness" being revealed to help humanity.

Mike George, Avoca, PA

About eight months ago I had a talk with Bob Butts, owner of CeeKay Auto in Moosic, Pennsylvania. When Bob discussed the "Water Cure" with me, I laughed. I really laughed. But, I had this leg problem. My legs used to swell up really bad. I could barely walk because of my arthritis and gout. I went to the doctor. He gave me anti-inflammatory pills. They just ended up ripping my gut out, so I stopped taking them.

Then, when Bob talked to me again about the Water Cure, I decided to start it. I have kept it going for the last four to six months. Now I feel like a young person. I am 54, but I feel like 20. I was ready to sell my business of 35 years and get rid of it. I figured that my legs were worn out. A least, that's what the doctors had told me. I needed joint, ankle, and knee replacements. I had one right knee done, but never went back for the left one. The first one didn't do any good.

My attitude changed greatly after I started drinking water. When you're living in constant pain, your mind is only on one thing. I was just going to get rid of the business and say I can't do what I used to do. I usually work 10 to 15 hours a day. I felt I might as well get out of the business. Then I started just drinking water and adding a little salt on my food.

My health has really improved in the last four to six months. Since I have been following the Water Cure, I have made it a habit. When I talk to people about this, they laugh at me. Well, I laughed at it in the beginning, too. Now, I don't take any pills. My joint pain is just about gone.

It is funny, people with swollen legs are told not to drink so much fluids and to stay away from salt, but I did the opposite and my legs are just about down to normal.

Before I started on the Water Cure - on a scale from one to ten (best being ten), I felt like checking out... a zero. I wanted to die, but now, at least, I am a seven or eight. When I get to ten, I'll let you know.

Michael V. Krol, Honesdale, PA, 570-253-2259

My life changed after two months on the Water Cure. As the result of an accident in 1954, I suffered a broken back, dislocated shoulder, dislocated knees, a smashed foot and a fracture skull. I've had severe pain and discomfort ever since. I was taking Lasik, a diuretic, for edema of both legs. I also took lisinopril for high blood pressure and was told to use no salt. I was a heavy consumer of alcohol most of my life. It got to where I was drinking one or two six-packs of beer each day, and sometimes as much as a full case. I prayed to God to help me stop drinking.

I first heard about the Water Cure on "Positive Press on the Air." My wife and daughter went to Cee-Kay Auto and spoke to Bob Butts about the Water Cure. I sat in the car. It wasn't easy for me to come in.

I read the literature and it made sense to me, so I tried the Water cure. The day I started drinking a gallon of water a day, I quit drinking alcohol. I've had no desire for any since, even when in the company of others drinking alcohol. My pain is diminished to the point I don't park in handicap spots.

I am now off of all pain medication. The edema in my ankles disappeared in two days. In two weeks my blood pressure returned to normal, and I've been off of the medication since.

My 45 years of broken back pain was gone in two months. My energy also improved. It's incredible how much my life changed for the better in just two months.

Nancy

I must tell you the story of my friend, Bob, for the benefit of others. He was concerned about edema in his feet and legs, and was taking Lasix and not drinking water. I tried to tell him that edema is the body's attempt to hold on to what little water there is, and he needs more water, not less. I pointed out that every cellular process in the body depends on water.

He never got it.

In 1999 I went to visit him and he, looking like a prune, proudly showed me his legs. "I finally got all the water out of my feet," he said. I asked him if he was drinking water. He held up an eight-ounce glass. "I'm sipping it," he said. I gathered he was going to make that glass of water last as long as possible. Again, I told him he must drink water.

Less than 24 hours after telling me he got "all the water out of his feet," he went to the hospital, where they declared he had dehydrated himself so thoroughly that his heart, liver an kidneys were damaged beyond repair.

His second day in the hospital he felt wonderful, getting hydrated again, and I told him that if he didn't drink water, he could become so dehydrated that his heart was trying to pump dust. He finally got it. But it was too late. He died September 10, 2009. He was 75.

Nina Razor, Dietitian and Diabetes Educator, Atlanta, GA
Hi, Bob: Thanks for your advice through this web site. My legs and feet had been swelling for almost two months, and my doctor couldn't find anything wrong. He finally gave me diuretics. Another doctor told me, "Don't worry. Women swell."

Thank God I read the testimonials about edema. I began with the Water Cure. Five days later I had no swelling, and I feel more relaxed and with more energy. I am working out harder and I am delighted.

I am a dietitian. I read all of the scientific work on this Water Cure and I loved it! Keep up the good work!

Tom LaBresh
I'm sure my son, Tom, has no idea of what he did for me when he first sent me Dr. Batmanghelidj's information about sea salt and water.

In mid-May, my right ankle began to swell and became quite large. The only thing I knew to do was to take a diuretic. After that, I went up and down like a yo-yo.

As Memorial Day and our trip to Big Bear approached, it kept getting much worse. I went to my doctor and he had a great idea... double the dose of Lasix. He warned me that my ankle would only get worse at the 7,000-foot elevation in Big Bear. It did. Fortunately, he buffered the Lasix with potassium.

Then, in mid-July, Sally was having some problems with swollen ankles. Phyllis also was having the same problem. I told them to get a diuretic and double the dose.

Then came your information about the Water Cure and sea salt. I began doing it immediately - drinking half my weight in ounces of water every day. My swelling came down immediately, and I quit the Lasix right away.

What I found out from Dr. Batmanghelidj was that a diuretic drains water out of the body and can cause serious dehydration. He said the best diuretic in the whole world is just plain water.

I see the results in my own foot, and I shudder to think of what might have happened had I gone on with what I was doing. I also feel bad because I was trying to tell Sally and Phyllis to take more diuretic.

My ankle is all healed. The timing of Dr. B.'s information was so perfect. I think God used my son to help me keep from making a terrible mistake.

Terri and Gino Kollar, terrikollar@gmail.com,
Hi Dr. Bob,

It has been five months since our last correspondence. If you remember, my husband was very sick and was blown up with edema. He had pulmonary hypertension, edema (of approximately 40lbs), low blood count (hemoglobin), low iron, he's on oxygen (COPD), hep c,(bad liver), neuropathy in hands and feet, high blood pressure and heart-rate, and a few more things to boot.

Last time I wrote to you, we had already started taking the sea-salt with the water routine, weighing on the cautious side, and it was already trying to clean out his lungs, (bringing up a lot of phlegm). We then moved into the chlorophyll, of which we decided to go with the chloroxygen gel caps instead of the liquid form. We take two with orange juice, then the salt water in the morning. In the last five months, my husband lost all of his edema, (from 156 lbs to 180 lbs). He does still take a little lasik everyday because his heart is enlarged to three times its' original size on the left side. (He went without lasik for three days due to prescription delay), and his feet started to swell again slowly. So we know his heart isn't quite strong enough yet. Anyway, he is no longer on any of his blood pressure medicine.

His stats usually read 118/65 with his hr anywhere between 76 and 90. We are thrilled with his progress and right now his iron is only 3%, but he is getting veneral once-a-week (iron shots). He had a bleed they could not find until six months ago. They stapled it and it came apart again, so he has four staples in a duoduin vein. Once his iron comes back up, his oxygen will get better and believe we will be getting him off his oxygen eventually.

Before I knew of you, Dr. Bob, and the Water Cure, my husband was on 12 medications everyday. The Water Cure now has him down to six meds a day. I believe with all my heart that if it would not have been for the Water Cure, my husband would no longer be with me. I know the only way to thank you is to spread the word, of which I do as often as I possibly can!

Thank you Dr. Bob, for your taking time out of your busy day to write personally to me. It really helped me to feel like I was not alone in my quest to get my man better.

> **Message from Bob Butts:** I am not a doctor, just a friend who loves passing on what I have learned from Dr. B. I wish doctors were trained in the Water Cure, as it would cut health costs to almost nothing. That's because water and salt are the most life-essential nutrients, and if a person is deficient in either, it is impossible to have good health. I believe that the main reason profit-driven businesses do not accept it is because there are no incentives to eliminate high-profit problems because money is valued more than people. That is especially true since the Water Cure works, it's free, and nobody can make a cent on it.

Edema: A Final Word

As you now know from the above testimonials, edema must not be treated with diuretics, since edema drains fluid from the entire body into the affected parts. The body then reacts by urgently requiring replenishment of that fluid rather than depletion of it. Your Body's Many Cries for Water" for full explanation.

> **Message from Bob Butts:** Most people who do any flying at high altitudes know that the ankles often swell, and the crew knows that all a person needs to bring them down is to drink water.

WATER CURE PROTOCOL

Instructions and Nutrition **including:**

- 👍 **Important tips to know before starting**
- 👍 **Dr. Batmanghelidj's recommendations**
- 👍 **There are four ways to take the salt**
- 👍 **Caution on swelling**
- 👍 **Water should stay within your body 2-3 hours**
- 👍 **Something to stop**
- 👍 **Daily food requirements**
- 👍 **Suggested supplements**
- 👍 **What to expect**
- 👍 **Exercise**
- 👍 **If you do not get the results you expected**
- 👍 **Quick Reference: Water and Salt Intake**

WATER CURE DIRECTIONS AND NUTRITION

Important tips to know before starting the Water Cure Program:

👆 Water should stay inside your body for 2-3 hours so your body has time to use the water properly.

👆 You must be sure your kidneys are working okay. This means liquid in results in liquid out. For example, the amount of water or other beverages taken in should be urinated during the day.

Here are Dr. Batmanghelidj's recommendations

- The "rule of thumb" for water is half your body weight in ounces taken throughout the day. A little less or even a little more is okay.

- If you have any swelling of your feet, ankles, legs, arms, fingers, eyelids, you must stop all salt for 2 or 3 days and just drink the water. The exception to this would be swelling from an injury/accident.

You probably rolled your eyes to the back of your head saying, "Are you nuts? That's a lot of water to drink." Actually, it's quite simple to accomplish this when taken in, say, 8 glasses of water spaced throughout the day.

For example, let's take a 192-pound person. Half his/her body weight is 96 pounds. Change that to 96 ounces. Divide that by eight for the number of glasses you are going to drink, which equals 12 ounces per glass. You would be drinking eight 12-ounce glasses per day. Now... wouldn't you say that drinking the water this way is easy to do?

If you do not drink that much water right now, you must start adding the extra water very slowly. This gives your body time to adjust to the added water intake. If you don't, the water will act like a water pill (diuretic) pulling necessary minerals from your body, possibly causing more harm than good. **Senior citizens and children MUST start adding the extra water slowly.**

Here's how to increase your water intake slowly. Using the above example, start out with three 8-oz glasses of water your first day. The next day add one or two glasses. Keep doing this until your "required-glasses-per-day" is reached. Now start increasing the ounces until your total per glass is reached.

Please keep in mind, it's only a "rule of thumb" on half your body weight in ounces of water and 1/8 teaspoon of salt for every 16 ounces of water. Some people will require a little more water, where others will require a little more salt.

After a while, the body's requirements can change for a little more water and salt because of hot weather, cold weather, or exercise. Each person must find his or her body's requirement at this time.

Never drink more than 33.8 ounces (one liter) of water maximum at one time (or sitting).

- Children ages two and up will need 75% of their body weight in ounces of water per day, because their bodies are growing all the time and every cell in their expanding body needs this extra water (mytosis).

- Children who are active or playing sports can require up to 100% of their body weight in ounces of water per day.

- The Water Cure program does not apply to newborns up to two years of age.

There are four ways to take the salt.

Iodized table salt will work in a pinch, but unrefined non-oven-dried sea salt is best because of the extra trace minerals found in it. Sea salt also tastes better. There are four ways to take the salt:

1. The best way is to just dissolve the salt on your tongue - let it dissolve as much as you can and drink the water after the salt, washing it down.

2. If you are very salt-sensitive, then you would get some empty capsules and put the amount of salt you require into the capsules and take it with food.

3. When you put some salt on your food, be careful not to overdo it. If you use too much in addition to dissolving it on your tongue, you will acquire a taste for very salty food.

4. When ill or having a problem, you can do a "quick fix" by dissolving 1/8 teaspoon of salt in eight ounces of water. Swish, gargle and spit one mouthful of the salt water at a time and swallow just the last mouthful.

Please note that it is not advised to drink salt water for a continued period of time. DRINKING SALT WATER CAN CAUSE FURTHER DEHYDRATION.

You must also make sure you are getting at least 350 mcg of iodine in your multi-vitamins each day, up to a maximum of 450 mcg of iodine each day.

You may want to look at www.drbrownstein.com. Dr. Brownstein further researched Dr. Batmanghelidj's teaching that "we require iodine since there is none in sea salt." This research is very interesting and informative.

You need to read the "histamine article" on the web site watercure2.org so you can better understand how to tell when you need more salt, more water or more potassium (which is found in most foods).

It is very important for you to have one of Dr. Batman's books. A suggestion would be *"ABC of Asthma, Allergies and Lupus"* or his latest book, "Obesity, Cancer and Depression." The ABC book contains a lot more than what the title states.

There are six pages in each book on why a person needs salt and what it does in the human body.

Caution on Swelling

If you have any swelling of your feet, ankles, legs, arms, fingers, eyelids or excessive diarrhea, **you must stop all salt for 2-3 days.** Just drink the water. The exception to this would be swelling from an injury-accident. **Note:** Too much salt can cause diarrhea.

Then begin taking the salt again, but add it back slowly. You should use no more than 1/8 teaspoon (3/4 g) of salt per 16 ounces (½ liter) of water.

Dr. Batman says drinking plain water by itself will flush out all of the extra salt the body was holding in the cells and help clean out the system. The water will run through you very quickly pulling very important minerals from the body. It is suggested that you take a multi-vitamin with all three main meals to replace what minerals might have been pulled out.

When the swelling is gone, you can restart the program of drinking half your body weight in ounces of water. This time, however, you will take it in small amounts throughout the day, slowly increasing the amount of water until up to half your weight in ounces of water has been reached. Also, start taking the salt with the water.

You must also make sure you are getting at least 150 mcg of iodine in your multi-vitamins each day, up to a maximum of 450 mcg of iodine each day.

Water should stay in your body 2-3 hours.

This is so your body has time to use the water properly. If you are urinating sooner than 2-3 hours after drinking your water, you should stop drinking plain water and switch to drinking orange juice, lemonade, grape/cranberry juice, or any other juice. One point of caution. Asthmatics should never drink orange juice.

Note: When drinking orange juice, you should add 1/8 teaspoon of salt per eight ounces.

If drinking juice does not work, the next thing to try is experimenting with drinking your juice while eating a bagel. This means:

- Drink and eat the bagel at the same time... OR

- Eat the bagel first. Then drink your juice.

- Optional - increasing the salt to 1/4 teaspoon of salt per eight ounces when you are eating the bagel. The bagel may help retain the water longer.

You can put cream cheese, real butter or jam on the bagel. Afer using a whole bagel for a day or two, then you can cut down to using half of a bagel, then a quarter and just stop the bagel and use your food to take with the juice.

Here is how you should slowly go from drinking juice to going back to drinking plain water again. After a few days, you should try drinking two ounces of plain water a half hour before eating food. Then you can increase the water to four ounces a half hour before eating food. Next it should be six ounces, then eight ounces, and so on until you get up to the required amount.

Water should stay inside your body for 2-3 hours so your body has time to use the water properly. (See *"Water Cure Tips"* under *"Critical Water Cure Information"* at www.watercure2. org and www.watercure.com)

Something to stop

<u>CAFFEINE</u>

- Robs the body of vitamins B-1, B-2, vitamin C, zinc, potassium & other important minerals
- Interferes with DNA replication (how cells repair and reproduce in the body)
- Can be highly toxic (the lethal dose estimated to be around 10 grams)
- Can interfere with learning and memory (ADD - Attention Deficit Disorder)

Daily intake adds up over a year. Caffeine accumulates in the body's fat tissues and is not easily eliminated. The amount of caffeine that is staying in the body depends on the amount of caffeine intake. One cup of coffee contains an average 80 mg of caffeine. Mountain Dew soda has 120 mg. Starbucks 8 oz. coffee has 160 mg.

Read more about caffeine in the following books by Dr. B.: "ABC of Asthma, Allergies and Lupus" - pgs 166-168

"Water for Health, for Healing, for Life" - pgs 227-230

Suggested daily supplements

Acidophilus, or a good pro-biotic - Good bacteria needed by intestines. Take one with each meal (pill form).. 4 billion pill is best.

Beta Carotene - Eat one or two medium raw carrots, with skin, per day.

B-6 - 100mg after breakfast and evening meal. The body uses up B-6 every day.

Zinc - 50mg after breakfast and evening meal. This is for stress. The body uses up zinc everyday. Males also take 50mg after noon meal. When body is low in zinc, it borrows it from the prostate.

Vitamin C 500mg after breakfast, lunch and evening meal. Time-released with rose hips are best.

Flax Seed Oil - 6-9 grams. Two capsules after breakfast, lunch and evening meal. This does not apply to young children or to the underweight elderly.

Multi-Vitamin - Take one good multi-vitamin tablet 2 times a day or Swanson whole food multi-1 three times daily with meals.

Kelp (Iodine) - 150mcg - 1 per day if it is not in your multi-vitamin.

Chlorophyll - Take 1 tablespoon of liquid -3 times daily. You can buy De Souza's liquid chlorophyll at a low cost from www. vitacost.com. Chlorophyll morning and evening, or Swanson Vitamins chlorophyll capsules.

Daily Food Requirements

At breakfast, lunch and evening meal, choose one of the following food groups:

Eggs – At least two eggs every day. If sick, four or more eggs (raw, hard-boiled, poached, scrambled, etc.).

Beans - red, white, kidney, pinto, green, lentils, lima.

Nuts - 1 or 2 handfuls - pecans, walnuts, almonds, cashews, or brazil nuts.

Cottage cheese (4%)

Yogurt - Yoplait Original or Stonyfield are the best. Do not use artificial sweeteners.

Now add the following two food groups:

Fresh fruits - cantaloupe, apple, peach, pear, nectarine, melon, banana, etc.

Fresh vegetables - broccoli, green beans, snow peas, celery, carrots, squash, cabbage, etc. (raw, sliced broccoli stems with dressing OK)

What to Expect

Going to the bathroom after one week of doing the water and salt - your stool will become light yellow/brown or light green, float, have little odor and can be 1-2 feet in length. You should be using very little paper.

Going to the bathroom (#1) will have little color except after eating meats or taking vitamins. You will be going #1 a lot, but the time will get longer in between visits to the bathroom. Water taken first time in the morning will be passed quickly.

If your eyelids, ankles or fingers swell, then you're getting too much salt. Drink your next couple of glasses or bottles of water without taking salt. Suggestion: When you restart the salt, reduce a little from the original amount. However, if you get muscle cramps, you need salt. Add a little salt to your fruit or take extra salt on your food.

Exercise

Walk morning and evening (mall, treadmill, around the block)

Get at least 15 minutes of sunlight 2 times a day. Expose as much skin as possible.

You should strive to drink at least one 8-oz. glass of orange juice every morning. "No pulp" and "not from concentrate" is the best. You need 1/8 teaspoon (3g) of salt per 8-oz. orange juice so that your body can utilize the potassium in the orange juice.

(If a person has any breathing problems such as asthma, he or she should limit the orange juice intake to one, at most two, glasses a day.)

NOTE: If you're tired, take a glass of water and eat some salt. If you still feel tired 10-15 minutes later, then take a glass of orange juice with salt as described above. Any time you feel you need water, drink some. If you feel hungry (when it's not your scheduled time to eat), first drink some water and eat the salt and wait ½ hour. If you still feel hungry, have something to eat

If you do not get the results you expected

Different individuals have different water and salt needs depending on urination, blood pressure and swelling. Listen to Biser/Dr. B's interview; read critical water cure and salt information, and read appropriate testimonials.

Quick Reference - Program for Water and Salt Intake

This information comes from the books of F Batmanghelidg, M.D.

The formula for water intake is half your weight in ounces of water divided by five or six for the number of times you can drink the water throughout the day and the size of the container or amount of water you drink each time. IMPORTANT: When you drink your water, get it down to 5-6 minutes. Don't nurse it.

EXAMPLE: For a 300 pound person - half is 150 ounces divided by five, or a 30-ounce bottle. Use a 32-ounce bottle five times a day or a 24-ounce bottle six times a day.

SALT: Sea salt is best. It has one of the highest mineral content. Use a measuring teaspoon. The rule of thumb is to dissolve on your tongue 1/16 teaspoon for every eight ounces of water you drink, 1/8 teaspoon of salt for every 16 ounces of water you drink, , 1/4 teaspoon for every 32 ounces (one quart) you drink, or ½ teaspoon for every 64 ounces you drink, or one full teaspoon for every gallon you drink. (Some people will need less salt; others more.)

Remember not to drink more than 33 ounces at any one time when you drink. This is a starting point, not a set rule. Your dose of water and dose of salt will vary by whether or not you hold urine two hours after drinking. You can also, in addition, salt your food to taste.

NOTE: ONLY add ½ teaspoon of salt to eight ounces of water if you are using a "quick fix" described on the front web site page - shake or stir it. The best way to use salt is to just place the salt onto your tongue - let it dissolve, then drink water.

Message from Bob Butts: All information in this section was edited from Dr. Batmanghelidg's books by Mr. Jim Bolen, an associate of Dr. B. Please visit the site or mail watercure2.org, 4949 Birney Avenue, Moosic, PA 18507 with any questions concerning the Water Cure Recipe or the Nutrition Table.

WATER CURE HISTORY

WATER CURE HISTORY

From "Back to Eden" - Jethro Kloss

Water has been used from time immemorial for remedial purposes. The world's oldest medical literature makes numerous references to the beneficial use of the bath in treating various diseases. The learned Greek, Hippocrates, who lived about five hundred years before Christ and is referred to as the "father of modern medicine," was the first to write much on the healing of diseases with water. He used water extensively, both internally and externally, in treating illness of all kinds.

"When pain seizes the side, either at the commencement or at a later stage, it will not be improper to try to dissolve the pain by hot applications. A soft large sponge, squeezed out of hot water and applied, forms a good application. A soft fomentation like this soothes pains, even such as a shot to the clavicle."

Hippocrates goes on to say, "....for the bath soothes the pain in the side, chest and back, concocts the sputa, promotes expectoration, improves the respiration, and allays lassitude, for it soothes the joints and the outer skin, and is diuretic, removes heaviness of the head, and moistens the nose. Such are the benefits to be derived from the bath."

Long before Hippocrates recorded his experiences with the healing properties of water, we had learned from the study of ancient history that the Egyptians enjoyed bathing in their sacred river, the Nile. Pictures of ancient Egyptians, found in the tombs, show people preparing for a bath. The baby Moses was found in the rushes when Pharaoh's daughter went down to the river to bathe. Bathing held a prominent place in the instructions that were given by Moses, under divine guidance, for the government of the Hebrew nation.

The relations of the bath to the treatment of leprosy would lead us to believe that it as used for its curative effects, and it would seem likely that an agent held in such high regard as a useful remedy would also be highly esteemed as a preventive of disease.

The ancient Persians and Greeks erected stately and magnificent public buildings devoted to bathing. The baths of Darius I (about 558-486 B.C.), one of the earliest Persian kings, are spoken of as being especially remarkable.

The Greeks were probably the first nation to use the bath for personal cleanliness as well as for health reasons. Records show that they were using the warm bath more than one thousand years before the birth of Christ. In the ruins of King Nestor's palace in Greece there was found a built-in bathtub and drainage system more than 3000 years old. Rome, however, surpassed all of the older nations in the costliness and magnificence of the bathing facilities. The first public bath was erected in Rome in the year 3123 B. C. and used only cold water.

It was not long, however, until warm water baths replaced all those using cold water alone. Some of the greatest works of architecture in Rome were the warm public baths, which were supplied with every convenience for increasing the use and luxury of bathing as well as having many rooms for social gatherings. Kings and emperors each endeavored to construct a larger and more ornate public bath than their predecessors. The baths of Diocletian, completed in 302 A.D., were the largest in the world and could accommodate up to 10,000 bathers at the same time. It took 10,000 Christian slaves nearly seven years to complete their construction . When the baths were completed, the slaves had the choice of renouncing their religion or suffering martyrdom. At one time the number of public baths in Rome reached nearly one thousand.

Two noted physicians of the Roman Empire, Celsus and Galen, praised and glorified the bath as being invaluable for the treatment of a number of specific diseases. Galen said that exercise and friction must be used with the bath in order to have a perfect cure. If only the physicians through the following centuries had continued the practice of Galen, as described in his works, what a lot of suffering would have been avoided. Doctors would have refreshed and revived their fever-stricken patients with the use of God-given water, instead of giving them drugs like quinine, mercury, arsenic, etc., and letting them be consumed by fever that parched their lips and disorganized their blood. The Emperor Augustus was said to have been cured by water remedies of a disease that had resisted all other methods of treatment.

The Arabians have sometimes been looked upon as a wandering horde of wild men, but about one thousand years ago they had physicians among them that were some of the most learned men of that age. They were very sensible and enthusiastic about the benefits of the bath. Rhazes, one of the most prominent among them, described a method that is scarcely outdone by present-day water treatments. Baths were also used during pestilences. In Constantinople, Turkish baths were very popular during the fifteenth century.

In the year 1500 A.D., public vapor baths were numerous in Paris, France. They were connected with the barber shops, as many still are in that country at the present time. Dr. Bell, of Paris, states that in connection with the city hospitals, nearly 130,000 baths were given in a single year to outside patients. Undoubtedly, patients in the hospitals were steamed and bathed as well. What a marked contrast with present-day hospitals in this country where the use of water treatments is most sadly neglected. Such neglect is inexcusable.

The Germans in olden times were very fond of bathing. According to the records of history, during the Middle Ages when there were many cases of leprosy, it was a religious duty to bathe because of the national faith in bathing. History also tells us that Emperor Charlemagne, who was a giant of a man over seven feet tall with long blond hair, held court while relaxing in a huge warm bath.

During the early part of the eighteenth century, water was used medicinally. Floyer published a history of bathing in which remarkable cures were reported, and he recommended the bath for numerous diseases. A Mr. Hancock, who was a minister, published in 1723 a book called *"Common Water, the Best Cure for Fevers."* Another book, whose author is unknown, was called *"Curiosities of Common Water."* It was also published in 1723. In this book, water was said to be an "excellent remedy which will perform cures with very little trouble, and without charge, and may be truly styled a universal remedy." French and German writers were also advocating the use of water as a remedy during this same time.

In the early part of the nineteenth century, Vincent Priessnitz popularized the use of cold water as a curative measure. He was a peasant who lived in the Austrian part of Silesia from 1799 to 1851. In the small Austrian town where he grew up, water was used by the people to treat many ailments. When only a young man, Priessnitz suffered a severe injury. Several of his ribs were broken and his chest was caved in on the left side by a loaded wagon. Several of his teeth were also knocked out. The doctors who came to see him did not offer any hope for a cure. But he remembered several years before when he had successfully treated a badly-crushed finger by holding it in cold water until the bleeding stopped and the pain was relived, and he decided to treat his broken ribs in the same way. So by taking deep breaths while leaning over a chair to expand his ribs and using cold water, he was gradually completely cured.

It was not long after this that Priessnitz began to use this cold water treatment on others. His routine course of treatment consisted of cold baths and compresses, along with friction. He used this form of treatment for all manner of disease, since this was what had cured him. He combined the cold water therapy with exercise, deep breathing, and a diet of dark bread, meat, and vegetables that he grew in his own garden. His success greatly encouraged him, but he met with considerable opposition from the doctors when he treated some of their patients and cured them, after the doctors had given them up.

Although Priessnitz had no formal education, he developed various ways of applying cold water to the body to treat different diseases. His fame increased rapidly and in a few years he was known throughout the world. Today he is called the father of modern hydrotherapy. He succeeded in restoring hundreds of people to health who had been pronounced incurable. His friends claimed that he was a great discoverer, but he really didn't discover anything that had not been known for at least a century, if not for thousands of years before.

A famous neurologist in Vienna, Dr Wilhelm Winternitz, went to observe Priessnitz's Water Cure treatment center in Graefenberg, Austria. He was so impressed with what could be accomplished with such simple means that he spent the rest of his life working to develop new methods of water treatment. The influence of Dr. Winernitz was felt by such well-known American Water Cure advocates as Dr. Simon Baruch and Dr. John Harvey Kellogg. It was Dr. Baruch who was chiefly responsible for the passage of laws in the state of New York that required the establishment of municipal baths in that state. Dr. Kellogg was the director of the Battle Creek Sanitarium in Michigan, the largest hydrotherapy treatment center in the United States, until it was destroyed fire on February 18, 1902.

He developed many new treatments, including the electric light bath that used natural methods.

The Water Cure spread to America about 1850 and until 1854 it prospered greatly, but most of the doctors were opposed to this treatment. It seemed almost as though they did not want the people to get hold of any remedy that was practical, inexpensive, and could be used in any home. About 1870 they successfully had a law passed that prevented the Water Cure practitioners from practicing in New York. Since New York City was the headquarters, as soon as these treatments were stopped there, their use was abandoned nearly everywhere for a while.

Sebastian Kneipp, a Catholic priest in Bavaria who cured Archduke Joseph of Austria of Bright's disease during the late nineteenth century, gained a wide reputation because of his success with the Water Cure. He also had the patients return to nature, as far as possible. He used herbs with great success because he combined their use with other natural remedies.

The North American Indians used bath for many diseases. They developed original ways of giving both water and vapor baths. The vapor bath was the most commonly used, and it was followed by a plunge into a cold stream. This is similar to the custom so widely practiced at the present time in Finland, of jumping into either the snow or ice-cold water following a hot sauna bath.

The native Mexicans also use a hot-air bath (sauna). They confine themselves in a brick house that is heated by a furnace located on the outside. They seem to have implicit confidence in the efficiency of the sauna bath to destroy disease, using it with much success when ill.

Water is one of the most powerful and yet one of the simplest remedies that can be used by an intelligent mother who understands the affects of hot and cold water on the body. If you cleanse and nourish your body properly, and leave nature to itself, it will renovate and heal the body.

Lately, people have been led to believe that there are remarkable virtues in certain spring waters (this refers to water from certain hot mineral springs that is used for external treatments). The claim that these waters are possessed of a miraculous healing power is not true. The healing virtue is in the moist heat that is obtained from the water.

Unfortunately, in the early days the reputation of water as a remedy was injured because people such as Vincent Priessnitz used it to extremes. Such practitioner did not understand the human body, the use of hot and cold water, or the useful and powerful reactions that are produced in the body when it is properly used. People were led to believe that it was a cure-all, and that cold water was the only remedy no matter what the condition of the disease might be. Rest, pure air, nourishing and simple food, sunlight, and exercise are of equal importance to water in all cases.

Although water is not a specific, it is one of the most valuable remedies. This is true not only of water, but also of other natural remedies. There may be a specific remedy for a particular disease, but there isn't a one-and-only remedy for every disease. Several remedial agents must be combined to suit the condition, and not a single one used to the exclusion of all of the others. But even so, water is an important agency in the treatment of nearly every disease when it is correctly applied and used with other forms of treatment.

> The whole thing in a nutshell is that the use of water, combined with an abundance of fresh air, sunshine, proper diet, exercise, rest, recreation and pleasant surroundings effects a cure. *Back to Eden, History of the Water Cure," by Jethro Kloss.*

KEY ISSUES

- 👍 **Dehydration Defined**
- 👍 **The Masks of Dehydration**
- 👍 **The Importance of pH**

DEHYDRATION DEFINED

Dehydration can be defined as "The body's excessive loss of water." It can be dangerous for life. Next to oxygen, water is number one in importance, as the body is 75% water. Salt is next. While doctors say salt is bad (which table salt is), unprocessed sea salt is extremely rich in vital minerals.

The human body constantly needs water. It loses water through the lungs, when breathing, and with the daily urination, sweat and stool.

The human body has many signals of its needing water, including the development of various pathologies, such as every health problem mentioned in this book.

Our bodies are 75% water, and the water inside our cells is salt-free, while the water outside our cells is salt water, which is the same as our planet. The water that surrounds our continent is all salt water, and the water within our continent is salt-free.

Body and planet are much alike, so why have doctors been taught to tell people that salt is bad when, in the middle ages, people were put to death by salt deprivation - a slow, agonizing death. I know one thing, and that is if people don't get enough unprocessed salt, their health could be impaired. Read critical salt information on the web site watercure2.org.

The dehydrated body needs the water, but it can refill it successfully only if there is enough salt in the body. Salt keeps the water in the body and normalizes the composition of the blood and intercellular fluid. When there is not enough salt, the water is removed from the body to keep salt concentration constant. After the cells receive enough water, they are not dehydrated any more, so the disorders caused by the dehydration can gradually disappear.

Therefore, first, all pain should first be treated by correcting any dehydration other than as in trauma pain. Almost all pain is not a mysterious disease. It is just dehydration alarm. The root cause of almost all pain is dehydration, which adversely affects every cell in the body. The pain we feel is from the acid burn that is present in severe dehydration. Read *"Your Body's Many Cries for Water"* to get the full understanding. The best book to start off with is *"Rx for a Healthier Pain-Free Life."* It is a complete overview of the Water Cure. Thus, all problems should first be checked for dehydration symptoms. Once corrected, most problems will disappear.

For the science of Dr. Batmanghelidj's Water Cure, also read *"Your Body's Many Cries for Water."* For a great Water Cure overview, read "Rx for a Healthier Pain-Free Life," packed full of life essential information. For many great testimonials and TV news specials, visit www.watercure2.org.

Message from Bob Butts: Doctors are taught to tell patients that salt is bad for them. Yet, in the middle ages, people were executed by salt deprivation because it was the most painful, agonizing death known to man.

THE MASKS OF DEHYDRATION

Many labels are given to various dehydration symptoms. A few of the more than 10,000 masks of dehydration are:

acid pH

acid reflux

ADD/ADHD

addiction

AIDS

amputation (the result of bad
circulation)

arthritis

asthma

back pain

birth defects

burning feet

cancer

cholera

cramps

depression

Diabetes

high cholesterol

Multiple Sclerosis

digestive problems

edema

kidney problems

much mental health

pregnancy

female & menopause
problems

fibromyalgia

gout

headaches

HBP

lupus

muscular dystrophy

obesity

R.S.D.

Suicidal tendencies

ulcers

many vision problems

Lou Gherig's Disease, Pain

THE IMPORTANCE OF pH

The article from which this excerpt is taken was written from personal experience and experience with clients, measuring pH with litmus paper, health results gathered over time, and such - not laboratory testing of isolated substances. *Your body pH affects every aspect of your health.*

The principles are clear: eat plenty of vegetables, some fruit daily, and don't eat too much of dairy products, grain products, and direct protein from eggs, meat and fish (as is typically the case in Western diet). Eggs are important but need to be minimized if you are allergic to them.

But remember... you *DON'T* have to cut out *all* acid-forming foods. Some are necessary, typically 40%. Otherwise you probably wouldn't get enough protein and variety of nutrients, let alone make interesting meals that you enjoy.

But you *DO* want to shift the overall balance of your diet over toward the alkaline, and away from the excessively acid-forming diet of a quick-food culture. The reason the Water Cure is so highly successful is that it restores the pH balance to our bodies so the body can heal itself.

Research shows that unless the body's pH level is slightly alkaline, the body cannot heal itself. So, no matter what means you choose to take care of your health, it won't be effective until the pH level is balanced. If your body's pH is not balanced, for example, you cannot effectively assimilate vitamins, minerals and food supplements. *Again, your body pH affects everything.*

Follow this link for a free alkaline diet guide and recipes, plus a full-Acid-Alkaline food chart.

Http://acidalkalinediet.com/foodchart.php?file=29

Also, additional information is available from:

http://trans4mind.com/recommended/?ph

RESOURCES

- 👍 **Contacts**
- 👍 **Articles**
- 👍 **Diskettes**
- 👍 **Books**
- 👍 **Web sites**
- 👍 **...and more**

RESOURCES

DISKETTES

These could be viewed, listened to, or copied from the following site:

Web Site: www.watercure2.org

> **_Listen to this disc first!!_**
> "Sam Biser Interview with F. Batmanghelidj, M.D."
> *[Proves that The Water Cure is the
> Greatest Health Discovery in History.]*

Disc One:
1. WYOU News Feature
2. WYOU Interview w/Bob Butts
3. WYOU Water Cure Documentary

Disc Two:
1. FOX TV Interview w/Bob Butts, Donna Riviello
2. Eye Witness News WJZ-TV, Ch 13 Baltimore 15 Water Cure Commercials Northeastern PA Testimonials

Disc Three:
1. WVIA PBS-TV Water Cure Fact or Fiction-Debate w/ Dr. R. Brown, Dr.. Batmanghelidj And Bob Butts.
2. Jeff Rense Interview with Bob Butts

Disc Four: Rescued From the Grave Testimonials covering 12 diseases

Disc Five: Testimonials covering diseases/conditions

Unnumbered Diskettes:
- Barry Farber Show, with the latest Water Cure news, featuring Bob Butts - 6/18/11
- Two-minute radio spots: 1. Water Cure Logic Wins All Star Game; 2. RSD walk fiasco, Alan Osmond; 3. RSD/ Todd Thorne testimonial
- Water Cure: Andrew Bauman
- Water: Rx for a Healthier, Pain-Free Life

Addresses for ordering full articles (see Media section):

Woman's World
DearWW@bauerpublishing.com

After Dark
Post Office Box 420-234
Palm Coast, FL 32142-0234

Crusader
Post Office Box 557
Black Mountain, NC 28711

Fit 4 Fishing
140 S. Barrington Ave., #353
Los Angeles, CA 90049

Harvard Health Review
One Jimmy Fund Way, Th 6
Boston, MA 02115
617-432-1000

Time Magazine
135 West 50th Street
New York, NY 10020
212-822-1212

www.watercure2.org
4949 Birney Ave., Moosic, PA 18507

Books by F. Batmanghelidj, M.D.

Your Body's Many Cries for Water
Water: Rx for a Healthier Pain-Free Life
Multiple Sclerosis: Is Water Its Cure?
Arthritis and Back Pain: Why They are the Same Disease
ABC of Asthma, Allergies & Lupus
Water: For Health, For Healing, For Life
Water Cures: Drugs Kill
Obesity, Cancer, Depression

[All books can be ordered from Amazon]
[See www.watercure2.org for complete list of Dr. B.'s works]

Woman's World Articles
–   Water: The New Immune Breakthrough
–   Bad Cholesterol: A Myth and a Fraud
–   Asthma Eradication Program
–   Cure Pain and Prevent Cancer
–   My Forever Healthy and Pain-Free Program
    [Google www.watercure2.org to read above articles.]
    [Google www.dearWW@bauerpublishing.com for these
    and other articles.]

Dr. B.'s *"Water: Rx for a Healthier Pain-Free Life,"* briefly reviewed below by Bob Butts, has been described as "a masterpiece" in a "quick-read" for the uninitiated in the value of the Water Cure in helping to save lives.:

WATER: RX FOR A HEALTHIER, PAIN-FREE LIFE

By F. Batmanghelidj, M.D.
[Review by Bob Butts]

O ver the years many doctors have endorsed the Water Cure only to be ignored because it challenged entrenched beliefs. *"Water: Rx for a Healthier Pain-Free Life,"* a self-education book by F. Batmanghelidj, M.D., will teach most how and why the Water Cure works.

The book starts with four pages of endorsements from medical doctors, medical newsletters, news stories from major newspapers, and medical schools that will convince most skeptics. Here's two examples:

- Hiten Shaw, M.D., said the Water Cure's easy to understand, and reading about it should be compulsory in all schools. It'll prevent lots of illnesses and suffering.

- Cardiologist Dan Roehm called the Water Cure revolutionary and sweeps nearly all diseases before it. It is a Godsend.

The Water Cure in this country can cause the paradigm shift we need to restore integrity in our health care system.

APPENDIX

- 👍 **Special Tribute by Alan Osmond**
- 👍 **The Water Cure and the Media**
- 👍 **Doctors In Support of the Water Cure**
- 👍 **Words from the Wise**

TO DR. BATMANGHELIDJ, WHO GAVE HIS WHOLE BEING TO GOD AND HUMANITY.

By Alan Osmond (of the Osmond Brothers)
February 21, 2011

F. Batmanghelidj, M.D.

I had an interesting experience with the people at www.watercure2.org as I read their information about the "Water Cure" and how water can "cure most ailments." I was intrigued enough to keep drinking water and even shared it here at The Family.com a few times. The other day, after communicating with Robert Butts of the Water Cure, I felt impressed to write a poem for them. I sent it to him and he requested back asking if he could share it with others. He told me that "Dr. B. is looking at me with a big grin because this poem is a tribute to all he has done for humanity. I wish you had known Dr. B. as I did, because he gave his whole being to God and humanity."

Message from Bob Butts: Alan's poem *is* a work of art.

I told him YES! Here is Bob's response, which I want to share with the world about a man who wants nothing more than to help humanity. This, and people like Dr. B., is what our world so badly needs!

–Alan Osmond

Bob and Connie Butts

"Thank you, again, Alan, for your faith and inspiration in Dr. B.'s water cure, and we who deliver his message. Truly it is from God. Dr. B told me, 'I have done nothing. I'm just God's messenger boy. I didn't discover water." He was always extremely humble. **Check his dedication in each book: 'To Our Creator: In awe with Humility, Dedication and Love.'** I believe he was and will always be one of humanity's greatest patriots.

"Ironically, without two of the world's worst enemies, the Water Cure may never have been born: Iran and the United States. Iran wanted him dead and that's why he was tried on 32 counts, each carrying the death penalty, and put in Evan prison. In his defense, he presented his papers on the water research that he did after treating his inmates at the prison, so if he were shot, the discovery would get out.

"After a two-week recess, the judge said, 'You have made a tremendous discovery, and we wish you good luck in the future.' That is how he found out he wasn't going to be shot. Because the revolutionaries destroyed all the materials he needed to continue his research, he escaped to the United States to continue his research. Dr. B. was given free access to everything at the University of Pennsylvania in Philadelphia, ironically founded by one of our greatest revolutionaries, Benjamin Franklin, to continue his research.

"Alan, I hope the legacy Dr. B. left us all will speed your complete recovery from MS and type 2 diabetes as we have seen most people quicky do. I'm sure, when your health is 100%, you will share the story of your recovery with the country and help people worldwide learn that there is no greater thing in life than experiencing the joy of making a difference in the lives of others.

"God bless you and your family, my friend, and may you continue to be great at being the kind of people with the values that create a better world."

–Bob Butts

"I'm pleased to honor Dr. B. for his discovery of using water as a 'Water Cure' but, more importantly, for where his heart was. Yes, he was a *'**Super Star of Goodness.**'* – Alan Osmond

THE WATER CURE

By Alan Osmond

Tears... from heaven as rain fills our streams,
Showers and baths, that help keep us clean,
Water for drinking's when good health begins
Baptized in water will wash away sins.

Each time you wash, or just walk past the sink,
Don't forget that your body ... needs a big drink.
Water helps sickness, but no one will tell, and
Doctors don't say much 'cause it makes you well.

Water is free and the cost is just right.
Drinking eight glasses a day... until night.
You'll feel much better; What stories you'll tell.
Health issues disappear, and you will be well.

It's a big secret, so don't say a word...
Unless you love others, then tell the unheard.
Water is the answer to help you endure.
Some even call it ... *The Water Cure.*

Alan Osmond and his wife Suzanne

WATER CURE AND THE MEDIA

- 👍 Including Excerpts from
   Related Articles
- 👍 Woman's World magazine
- 👍 After Dark magazine
- 👍 American Fisherman magazine
- 👍 Crusader newspaper
- 👍 Harvard Review
- 👍 Time Magazine
- 👍 The Times Leader
- 👍 The Citizens' Voice
- 👍 U.S. Centers for Disease Control & Prevention
- 👍 A Message from Barry Farber
- 👍 Radio Spots

THE "WATER CURE" CAN MAKE YOU THIN!

(Excerpts from *Woman's World* article)

"We can't rave enough about the latest weight-loss breakthrough. It's simple, safe and effective. This M.D.-devised technique has already worked wonders for All My Children's Finola Hughes, who shed 30 pounds three times faster than average—and without dieting" –Woman's World

Surprising reasons drinking water melts fat:

- Water makes your metabolism burn calories 3% faster. During a study at the University of Utah, test subjects who were just slightly dehydrated saw a 3% drop in their resting metabolism.

- **Water fights fatigue-induced hunger:** Studies have shown that the more tired we feel, the more we eat.

That's why folks who work the night shift tend to pack on extra pounds.

- **Water helps the digestive system operate more effectively,** so you have fewer cravings. The more water in our systems, the more efficiently our enzymes can break down and extract nutrients from food.

- **Water replaces beverages proven to cause weight gain:** It probably comes as no surprise that substituting water for sugary drinks saves you lots of calories. But what you might not know is that calories we drink are much more likely to end up as fat.

> **Message from Bob Butts:** The Water Cure has been a "Woman's World" cover story <u>five times</u>!

For more information, Google "Woman's World: The Slimming New Water Cure."

[Copies of the full article available from *Woman's World* (see "Resources" for address)]

> The average person drinks only 4.6 glasses of water each day. Doctors recommend eight 8-ounce glasses per day. "This chronic shortage is the reason so many of us are sick, tired, and overweight." — F. Batmanghelidj, M.D.*

THE WATER CURE

[Excerpts from *AfterDark* magazine article]

> "Can there be such a thing as a FREE cure-all that's available almost *EVERYWHERE?*" –Maureen A. Hennessy, *After Dark*

Yes. The free cure is water.

According to F. Batmanghelidj, M.D., known to his patients and those who stumble over pronunciation of this name as Dr. B., water is amazing.

Dr. B. was determined to scientifically prove that the human body produces pain when it is thirsty. .... Dr. B. published his findings in April 1985. Needless to say, this information was not well-received by the established medical community, or the drug manufacturers. Medical professionals have been educated to treat pain and disease with medications. Nowhere in their training as doctors are they taught what happens if one does not drink an adequate amount of water every day.

Dr. B. reports seeing water completely reverse conditions such as asthma, angina, hypertension, migraine, and arthritis pain... Colitis pain and chronic constipation, Chronic Fatigue syndrome, high cholesterol and obesity can also be successfully treated with nothing more than ordinary, clean tap water. It is only necessary to understand the problem.

Dr. B. believes this knowledge will make the practice of medicine simpler - and friendlier to you, your health, and your financial resources. What is more, medical jargon will no longer get in your way of understanding your own body and its ways of talking to you.

[Copies of the full article available from *After Dark* (*see "Resources" for address*)]

THE LESSONS OF ORAL
REHYDRATION THERAPY

*Excerpts from Harvard Public Health Review, Winter
2007 and Time Magazine European Edition, Fall 2006*

By Karin Kiewra

> Senior Lecturer, Richard Cash of HSPH - Harvard School of Public
> Health - passes on all he has learned about a simple solution to a global
> killer - Oral Rehydration Therapy.

HARVARD PUBLIC HEALTH REVIEW: We thought,
"This is great. We can all go home now."

But everybody didn't use it.

Lecturer Cash was talking about ORS - Oral Rehydration Solution - recently ranked No. 2 in a *British Medical
Journal* survey of the greatest health advances in the last 150
years. The simple elixir consists of **"a pinch of salt, a fistful of sugar, and a jug of water."**

To get ORS to the masses, researchers faced huge obsta-
cles, including: a medical culture that clung to IV therapy
as superior to what they considered a primitive form; a very

high prevalence of illiteracy, and no way to distribute ORS packets to remote areas.

Harvard School of Public Health has chronicled a ten-year effort to surmount these hurdles, and continue to use ORS to drive home a point that is as relevant today as it was years ago.

Through their efforts ORS has saved tens of millions of lives. For example, at a cost of a few cents, almost anyone alert enough to swallow can survive cholera, which can kill a man in four hours by draining him dry.

The work of Harvard continues, as they practice what they preach with onsite assistance by Lecturer Cash and others.

TIME MAGAZINE: In a cover story, *Time Magazine* reported that ORT (Oral Rehydration Therapy) has rescued at least forty million people from the grip of water and sewage-born pathogens since its adoption by the World Health Organization (WHO) in 1978.

Since then, WHO estimates, annual deaths worldwide among diarrhea's chief victims - children under age five - have plummeted from five million to 1.9 million.

[Karen Kiewra is the Associate Director of development communications at Harvard School of Public Health and editor of the Harvard Review.)

HYDRATE PROPERLY WITH A PINCH OF SALT

[Excerpts from *American Fisherman* magazine]

"This is from the magazine, *American Fisherman*. *It's the water cure recipe.*" –Bob Butts, watercure2.org

By Troy Lindner, *"Fit4Fishing, American Fisherman*

Next to breathing, water is the most important thing you can do for your body. You can survive many days without food, but only a couple without water. Every bodily function requires water, and perhaps nowhere is that more true than when you're fishing.

A simple guideline to follow: Divide your body weight by two and drink that number of ounces of water each day. For example, if you weigh 200 pounds, then you need 100 ounces of water per day. I weigh around 185 pounds and aim for two gallons a day, but I drink even more when fishing in hot weather.

I also add one or two pinches of unrefined sea salt (not processed white table salt) to my drinking water. The darker and more off-colored the salt, the better. Drinking too much water without a small percentage of salt isn't healthy.

The author of this article, Troy Lindner, has established successful careers as both a personal trainer and professional bass angler.

[Copies of the full article available from *Fit4Fishing, American Fisherman* *(see "Resources" for address)*]

WELLNESS SECRETS FOR LIFE

[**Excerpts from *Crusader* newspaper interview**]

Understanding the Link Between Minerals, Hydration, pH and Cell Health: Interview with A. True Ott, PhD

By *Crusader* Editor Greg Ciola

Crusader: Keeping the body properly hydrated with the right water is deeply connected to getting the right minerals into the body and into the right balance. Can you expound on water a little and tell us which kind is best and why?

A. True Ott, Ph.D.: *We humans are water beings.* We form during nine months in a water-filled environment called a womb. Our blood is water-based, as is our brains. Without water, minerals are worthless and vice versa. Without water, life on this planet would cease to exist - so I have a deep reverence for water. We consume water for one reason - HYDRATION - which means, we are consuming useable hydrogen ions primarily. Therefore, does it not make logical sense to choose the best water with the most free hydrogen ions available?

Here is a basic secret truth that is very, very, very misunderstood. *THE PURER THE WATER... THE MORE HYDROGEN IONS ARE AVAILABLE FOR THE CELLS.* In 1923, two chemists named Bronsted and Lowery designed a method for measuring the hydrogen content of water and other liquids. They called it parts or percentages of

225

hydrogen (pH) and designed a scale from 1-14 to measure the hydrogen content.

In measuring waters, they found that water can either be RICH in hydrogen ions or woefully deficient in them. Water that is rich in hydrogen measures 5 or 6 on the pH scale (acidic), while alkaline water is actually dehydrating. In my experimentation and research, there is a direct correlation with water purity levels and hydrogen content.

Thus, one should strive to consume the purest water possible - and that is simply steam distilled water.

[Copies of the full article may be obtained from *Crusader* (see "Resources" for address)]

This newspaper also did a special edition of interviews with Bob Butts and will be presented in a later edition of this book.

THE BATTLE FOR HEALTH IS OVER pH

[Excerpts from *Crusader* newspaper article]

Life and Death Hangs in the Balance.

By Greg Ciola and Gary Tunsky

Monitoring the body's pH levels and altering one's diet and supplement regimen in an effort to regulate it, may be controversial to a lot of doctors and scientists, but it has led to a paradigm shift in how some health care specialists are treating a variety of diseases successfully.

The study of pH and cellular terrain's involvement in human health dates back to the late 1800s to a famous French research scientist named Antoine Bechamp. ... Most doctors and scientists in Western medicine dismiss the fact that pH has anything to do with human health because the entire doctrinal theology of pharmaceutical-based medicine is built around Louis Pasteur's Germ Theory Of Disease ... which teaches that disease is best-managed by ... treating symptoms through a drug, cut, burn and poison method instead of looking at the entire patient's state of health and finding the root cause of a health problem and what can be done to fix it.

The pharmaceutical industry saw great potential for profits with Pasteur's work, and lots of healthy patients with Bechamp's. That's why we have a medical empire today that profits hundreds of billions dollars every year on "managing disease" instead of a health care revolution that brings true healing to humanity in a way that has never been seen before.

It can be proven beyond a shadow of a doubt that modern orthodox microbial medicine arose upon scientific error on the "kill" mode: kill the bacteria, kill the virus, kill the fungus, kill the tumor, and kill the cancer - **with the slow killing of the patient.** This doctrine has played a major role in the promotion of illness by creating resistant strains of germs and suppressing symptoms of illness, while the illness itself is left intact.

[Copies of the full article may be obtained from *Crusader* (see "Resources" for address) or from Bob Butts at watercure2.org.]

TOUTING THE 'CURE'

[Excerpts from "Times Leader Article"]

The Times Leader
Wilkes-Barre, PA
January 16, 2012

By Andrea Brookman

(Triumph Over Pain) features testimonials from people who claim "The Water Cure" helped them. *"If you're losing someone you love or they are very ill, why not try a free solution? You have nothing to lose."* Bob Butts

The (Water Cure) involves drinking enough water daily to equal half your body weight in ounces and using ¼ teaspoon of sea salt for each quart.

Bob butts, of Elmhurst, learned of the Water Cure in a book, written by Dr. Fereydoon Batmanghelidj, called *"Your Body's Many Cries for Water."* ... Butts has since taken the reins by promoting (Dr. Batmanghelidj's work) since Batmanghelidj's death in 2004. ... "The most critical elements to a powerful immune system are oxygen, water and salt," Butts said. ... Dr. Stephanie Cabello from Geisinger Wyoming Health Center, Plains Township (Pennsylvania), said that although water is essential to the body, she believes that the water cure can only work for certain ailments (and that) more research needs to be done. ...

"Triumph Over Pain" (based on the continuing and dedicated work of Bob Butts) is a tribute to the work of

Dr. Batmanghelidj, who dedicated the last 20 years of his life promoting public awareness of the healing powers of water. ... Harriet Clyde Kipps (Editor-In-Chief of *"Triumph Over Pain"*) first met Butts, owner of Cee Kay Auto Parts, a regional string of auto parts stores, while reopening a playground in her hometown village of Glen Lyon (Pennsylvania). ... Butts bought many of her children's books to help support her vision. ...

(Triumph Over Pain) provides testimonials from people who swear by the Water Cure and states that chronic dehydration (UCD) contributes to and even produces pain and many degenerative diseases that can be prevented and treated by increasing daily water and (sea) salt intake. ...

Butts has spent more than a half million dollars in his lifetime advertising what he believes is a free cure for nearly every illness. At his auto parts stores (in Northeastern Pennsylvania), he provides free information and video tapes. He also promotes additional information on his website, www. watercure2.org.

[For full article, Google: *Times Leader Wilkes-Barre PA Touting the 'Cure'*]

Bob Butts and Harriet Clyde Kipps

THE CLAIM: DRINKING MORE WATER CAN PREVENT MIGRAINES

THE EXAMINER
The Citizens' Voice
Wilkes-Barre, PA
HEALTH & SCIENCE 8/24/11
[from a New York Times article]

For migraine sufferers, summer can be a perilous time of year. Oppressive heat and spikes in temperature have long been thought to precipitate attacks in people prone to chronic headaches. One large study in the journal *Neurology* even showed that the risk of migraines jumps nearly 8 percent for every 9-degree rise in temperature.

But a simple step that may lower the risk, especially in warm weather, is to stay properly hydrated. Dehydration causes blood volume to drop, researchers say, resulting in less blood and oxygen flow to the brain and dilated blood vessels. Some experts suspect that a loss of electrolytes causes nerves in the brain to produce pain signals.

Anyone who has ever awakened dehydrated after a night of heavy drinking knows this feeling as a hangover. But migraine sufferers may be more sensitive to the effects of dehydration. In one study, also published in *Neurology*, scientists recruited migraine sufferers and divided them into two groups. Those in the first group were given a placebo medication to take regularly.

The others were told to drink 1.5 liters of water, or about six cups, in addition to their usual daily intake.

At the end of two weeks, the researchers found that those in the water group had increased their fluid intake by just four cups a day. But on average they experienced 21 fewer hours of pain during the study period than those in the placebo group, and a decrease in the intensity of their headaches.

To stay adequately hydrated, health officials recommend that men drink about 13 cups of liquid a day - from water, juice and other sources *(see Part Seven: Water Cure Protocol)* - and that women drink about 9 cups.

> **THE BOTTOM LINE:** *There is some evidence that proper hydration can help protect against high blood sugar, though more research is needed.*

See Chapter Six: Headaches

THE CLAIM: DRINKING WATER CAN HELP LOWER THE RISK OF DIABETES

THE EXAMINER
The Citizens' Voice
Wilkes-Barre, PA
HEALTH & SCIENCE 1/25/12
[from a New York Times article]

There are many reasons to stay properly hydrated, but only recently have scientists begun to consider diabetes prevention one of them. The amount of water you drink can play a role in how your body regulates blood sugar, researchers have found.

The reason: A hormone called vasopressin, which helps regulate water retention.

When the body is dehydrated, vasopressin levels rise, prompting the kidneys to hold onto water. At the same time, the hormone pushes the liver to produce blood sugar, which over time may strain the ability to respond to insulin.

One of the largest studies to look at the consequences was published last year in Diabetes Care, a publication of the American Diabetes Association. French scientists tracked more than 3,000 healthy men and women ages 30 to 65 for nearly a decade. All had normal blood sugar levels at the start of the research.

But those who consumed the most water, 17 to 34 ounces a day, had a risk roughly 30 percent lower than that of those who drank the least.

The researches controlled for the subjects' intake of other liquids that could have affected the results, mainly sugary and alcoholic drinks, as well as exercise, weight an other factors affecting health. The researchers did not look at eating habits, something future studies may take into account.

> **THE BOTTOM LINE:** *Research suggests that dehydration can increase the risk of diabetes.*

See Chapter Seven: Diabetes

SUGARY DRINKS AND OBESITY

U.S. CENTERS FOR DISEASE CONTROL & PREVENTION
EXCERPTS FROM THE REPORT BY MIKE STOBBE,
ASSOCIATED PRESS 9/1/11

Health officials say half of Americans drink a soda or sugary beverage each day - and some are downing an awful lot.

A new study found that one person in 20 drinks the equivalent of more than four cans of soda each day. *The Center for Disease Control and Prevention* research shows teenage boys drink the most soda, sports drinks and other sugary liquids.

Sweetened drinks have been linked to the U.S. explosion in obesity, and related health problems, health officials have been urging people to cut back. Some officials have proposed an extra soda tax, and many schools stopped selling soda or artificial juices.

But advocates say these efforts are not enough, and on August 30, 2011, a coalition of 100 organizations announced a new push. The effort includes the American Heart Association and some city health departments that plan to prod companies to stop selling sugary drinks on their property and at business meetings. - as Boston's Carney Hospital did in April, 2011.

There will also be new media campaigns, like the one started in Los Angeles that will ask: *"If you wouldn't eat 22 packs of sugar, why are you drinking it?"* *They hope through these efforts that drinking soda will become as unfashionable as smoking.*

THE BOTTOM LINE: *Dr. B's research over some 20 years has proven the adverse health effects of soda and other sugary drinks, and the positive health benefits of water...*

See Chapter Ten: Obesity

A MESSAGE FROM BARRY FARBER

CRN Digital Talk Radio and Talk Radio Network

Four innocent people, including the pharmacist, were gunned down in a Long Island pharmacy because of a crazed addiction to pain pills.

If you can accomplish anything material to fight pain, and I'm sure you can or you wouldn't be touting this book, *"Triumph Over Pain,"* I want to help.

I want to do commercials, which I will ask friends of mine who own some of their own commercial time to run, to sell the book. I'll be like my own "subcommittee" trying to line up talk shows for you on other stations and networks. The opportunity to lift lives here is limitless.

> Barry Farber was named "Talk Show Host of the Year" by the National Association of Radio Talk Show Hosts in 1991.

SAMPLING OF RADIO SPOTS AND INTERVIEWS ON THE WATER CURE

by Bob Butts

Radio Spot #1: Brown grass after a rain - "Look how unhealthy brown grass looks.... Yet, how fast it becomes healthy after a rain. The same is true for most terribly unhealthy people. Most are that way because we lack water, thanks to drinking caffeine, alcohol and soda that dehydrates us. "We are not sick, we are thirsty."

Radio Spot #2: Oral Rehydration Saves Lives - Learn how water and salt rescued 40 million people from death for just a few cents. Google "Harvard Health Review 40 million people rescued with water, salt, and sugar." Copy and show that report to your doctor! Medical science rejects this because there are no incentives in medicine, banking, auto parts, or any business to eliminate high profit problems. - Bob Butts

Radio Spot #3: Dear President Obama - The following radio spot, and others, will be aired nationally. If you would kindly Google "Harvard health review 40 million people rescued with water, salt, sugar, you would be amazed how oral rehydration has saved millions of live for pennies. But medical science rejects this because it is like most business, government and labor unions. There's more interest in money than helping people. Please discuss this Harvard Review with your staff so that action can be taken to correct this situation. I think all political contributions should no longer be taken from special interest groups that buy our government, which has created this mess. What do you think. Sincerely, Bob Butts

Radio Spot #4: Water-Cure Addiction by Barry Farber - Ninety-five percent of you will miss this commercial because of its...strangeness. The other five percent of you are very fortunate people. There's nothing to BUY here. It's all free. And, therefore, strange. An Iranian doctor, Dr. Batmanghelidj...he said, call me Dr. B...discovered the utterly unbelievable powerful healing powers of...WATER. That's all. WATER, with a touch of sea salt. The diseases that can be cured by Dr. B's WATERCURE are limitless...but the price you pay for this medicine is limited to, zero...water and maybe a few cents for sea salt. I would never read this headline – 45 years of alcoholism cured in 24 hours – if you had to pay even one dime. This is all free. Four innocent people murdered in a New York pharmacy because of addiction. When you go to watercure2.org...your life will lift. You'll see an unending range of medical conditions that can be cured with Dr. B's Watercure. Focus now...ADDICTION! The only one who can benefit from this commercial is YOU. And those close to you. You cannot pay one penny. It's free. Go to watercure2.org and get the whole range of the watercure possibilities, but, right now. We're talking about addiction. Go to watercure2.org...I'll repeat that twice more...and you will never kill anybody...and nobody who goes there will ever kill you. Addiction is so easily curable with the watercure. Nothing to pay. Everything to gain. Go to watercure2.org.

> **Message from Bob Butts:** To all in the news media who would like to interview Barry to find out why he puts his reputation on the line to promote the water cure, his email address is barryfarber@earthlink.net. He has interviewed F. Batmanghelidj, M.D., and me many times

Radio Spot #5: Failure-Proof Water Cure - Here is the fool-proof way to save our nation, our economy, millions of jobs, countless lives and 20 trillion dollars over ten years at no cost. First, make the creation of an ethical environment everywhere in our nation our #1 priority. People must be valued more than money and power in all we do. Watercure2.org testimonials prove why it's almost impossible for the Water Cure to fail because it addresses the cause, dehydration, and why medical science fails because it only addresses symptoms with drugs and procedures. See watercure2.org. Free CDs and loaner books at Cee-Kay Auto stores. –Bob Butts

Radio Spot #6: Health Problems - Have a health problem you cannot get rid of? Visit watercure2.org. That's watercure2.org. Learn how people worldwide get well at no cost after our trillion dollar medical science fails. More info: Google your symptoms and problem followed by no-cost natural solution. –Bob Butts

Radio Spot #7: High-Profit Problems - Every nation will continue to fail so long as we are so unethical we value money more than people. That is why governments, labor, financial institutions, medical science and business cannot solve high-profit problems. But when people are loved more than money, no nation can fail. –Bob Butts

Radio Spot #8: Public Service Message - Here's the irrefutable answer to all problems!! *Love people more than money*! If we did, the United States could not have 72nd best health record at #1 cost, as reported by the World Health Organization. *–The Water Cure, and C-K Auto Stores*

Radio Spot #9: Dear President Obama and The Salvation Army - Here is the simple answer to drug and alcohol addiction that you both know has been destroying countless lives and families. Recently, four people were gunned down in a pharmacy by a drug addict. This will eliminate the addiction driven cause. The reason it works so great is water detoxes completely and quickly. Nothing else will. Mr. President, I urge you to consider working with the Salvation Army, based on their expertise in addiction. I am airing this radio spot nationwide many times in the hope you and your staff will verify this simple truth. Read success stories on <u>watercure2.org</u>. This will not only save countless lives, cut 100 billion dollars a year in associated costs, but will save trillions on health costs, enough to pay off our national debt, fund reopening our manufacturing industry and restore millions of jobs. In a society peopled by individuals more concerned about being ethical than being rich, we would have almost none of the problems that we have today, especially unethical government and unethical business practices. There is a truth that says, "Winners prevent problems, losers try to make money on them." Lets start being winners. Live the "Golden Rule." - Bob Butts.

Notable Interviews Selected interviews with F. Batmanghelidj, M.D., by CBS, PBS-TV affiliates, New Hope TV (a Christian network in India), and others. Further information at sources online.

> Mike Adams interview witb Dr. Batmanghelidj
> Learn Why the USA has 72nd Best Health at #1 cost
> Critical Water Cure Information
> TV Testimonials Aired 12,000 Times
> Kindness Grants for School Kids

DR. B. AND THE WORLDWIDE WEB

Dr. B. sparked the interest of the web in instances too numerous to list here.. These are a few of the hundreds of interviews and reports covered on the web for those seeking more information about the doctor's work:

www.naturalnews.com/Report "The Water Cure: An Interview with Dr. Batmanghelidj"

www.watercure.com/Article_adams.html "Healing with Water: the work of ... Dr. Batmanghelidj"

www.alphabiotics.blogspot.com "The Water Cure: An Interview with Dr. Batmanghelidj"

www.curezone.com/foods/watercure.asp "The Water Cure recipe"

www.downarchive.com/a0a/da/ "Dr. Batmanghelidj: Health Miracles in Water and Salt..."

www.curezone.us/forums "Dr. F. Batmanghelidj at Water Forum: Water Cure..."

www.newresearchfindingstwo.blogspot.com "Water Cure: An Interview with Dr. Batmanghelidj"

www.curezone.com/Forums "Dr. Batmanghelidj on the Medicinal Effects of Water"

www.curezone.com/Forums "High Blood Pressure by Dr. Batmanghelidj"

DOCTORS IN SUPPORT OF THE "WATER CURE"

- 👍 Dan C. Roehm, M.D., F.A.C.P.
- 👍 Hiten shah, M.D.
- 👍 Edmund H. Handwerger, D.D.S., M.P.H.
- 👍 Perry A. Chapdelaine, Sr., M.A.
- 👍 Dr. Lorraine Day
- 👍 Dr. Julian Whitaker
- 👍 H.C. Purtzer, D.O.
- 👍 Dr. Majid Fadaie

DOCTORS IN SUPPORT OF THE "WATER CURE"

Comments on "Your Body's Many Cries for Water" by F. Batmanghelidj, M.D.

<u>Dan C. Roehm, M.D., F.A.C.P.</u> - "After having read many of Dr. Batmanghelidj's recent works, including his jewel of a book, 'Your Body's Many Cries for Water,' it is very apparent that this work is revolutionary and sweeps nearly all diseases before it. As an Internist/Cardiologist, I find this work incisive, trenchant, and fundamental. *This work is a Godsend for all.*" *Health Professional Review*

<u>Hiten Shah, M.D.</u> - "The author, as a result of the extensive clinical and scientific research, concludes that the body possesses many different thirst signals. Many different symptoms and signs of dehydration have until now been viewed as classical diseases of the body." *–Frontier Perspectives - The Center for Frontier Sciences at Temple University and San Jacinto MedicalCenter*

<u>Edmund H. Handwerger, D.D.S., M.P.H.</u> - "It is a well-written book and easy to understand. I think reading this book should be made compulsory in all the Elementary, Middle, and High Schools. It will prevent lots of illnesses and suffering at almost no additional cost."

<u>Perry A. Chapdelaine, Sr., M.A.</u> - "Dynamite! Your hypothesis is precisely the paradigm breakthrough that generates quantum leaps forward in disease etiology." *–Dr. Chapdelaine is Executive Director, The Arthritis Fund, The Rheumatoid Disease Foundation*

Dr. Lorraine Day - "Dr. Batmanghelidj's discovery regarding water was critical in my recovery. I could not have recovered without it." –*Dr. Day was a Orthopedic Trauma Surgeon at the University of California, Chief of Orthopedic Surgery at San Francisco General Hospital, and Associate Professor and Vice Chairman of Orthopedic Surgery at the San Francisco School of Medicine*

Dr. Julian Whitaker - "'Your Body's many Cries for Water" by F. Batmanghelidj, M.D., changed my thinking, and I believe that water is so good for you that drinking it is now one of the seven steps of the Whitaker Program." –*Developer of the Whitaker Program, "Health and Healing?*

H. C. Purtzer, D.O. - "Dr. Batmanghelidj's book is the best Health book I have read in 49 years of practice." –*Dr. Purtzer is a physician and surgeon*

Dr. Majid Fadaie - "Now I consider myself a lucky doctor that I was introduced to water therapy. My success rate has gone up many fold. I have been working with a variety of ailments, especially asthma, angina, intermittent cludication, arthritis and peptic ulcers, and the results are very promising."

WORDS FROM THE WISE

- 👍 **Richard T. Healy**
- 👍 **F. Batmanghelidj, M.D.**
- 👍 **Earthclinic.com Thailand**
- 👍 **Mayo Clinic**
- 👍 **Marcia Angell, M.D.**
- 👍 **Bob Butts**
- 👍 **Quotes from "Water: Rx for a Healthier Pain-Free Life"**
- 👍 **Pediatric & Adolescent Medicine**
- 👍 **Robert Wood Johnson Foundation**
- 👍 **Centers for Disease Control**
- 👍 **New York Times**

THE "WATER CURE" MAY WELL BE THE DIFFERENCE ...

Richard T. Healy, Executive Director
(Automotive Wholesale Association of
New England AWANE)

For fiscal year 1999, the AWANE medical insurance rates increased an average of approximately 14 percent. How does the independent businessman, meeting stiffer competition, working on reduced gross profits, incur additional increased medical costs as an employer? This continuous squeeze results in fewer medical benefits or ultimately no employer-sponsored medical program.

When the government gets into the act, the bottom line is always increased costs. Is there an answer? Yes, there is... people must take the responsibility for their own health. Ask 100 people, and 100 people, upon reflection, will tell you that "health is number one." Then, approximately 30% of the people will light up or drink excessively.

The medical industry can solve everything with a pill. There is always an easy and costly way, but despite our medical and technological progress, quality of life can disappear before the ultimate end. The "Water Cure" may well be the difference between a company sponsoring a health plan or, for economic reasons, dropping medical coverage.

The "Water Cure" is an act of war against a medical system which is absorbing approximately 14 percent of the gross national product. The "Water Cure"is a difficult marketing challenge because it costs nothing. Recognizing this, we must incorporate the "Water Cure" into our AWANE convention. We must give the"Water Cure" what it deserves. A great health plan helps people get better quicker.

ONE DISEASE - DEHYDRATION - WHICH CAUSES ACID pH & A WEAK IMMUNE SYSTEM. *ONE CURE* - HYDRATION AND ALKALIZATION.

F. Batmanghelidj, M.D.
[Google "Foods that Heal - Foods that kill!]

Before dehydration hurts you irreversibly, when your plum-like cells become prune-like, your body will show its urgent need for water through different types of pain. These pains are the newly-understood, drastic ways of showing dehydration. After much clinical and scientific research, my understanding is that the early indicators of acid burns in the interior of the cells and potential genetic damage that can take place are different forms and intensities of pain. Depending on the degree of dehydration, as well as the extent and the location of acid buildup inside the cells when a greater flow of water should have cleared the acid from that area

- the classic pains of the body are produced. They are angina pain, bulimia, colitis, dyspeptic pain, fibromyalgia, heartburn, lower back pain, migraine headaches, morning sickness due to pregnancy, rheumatoid joint pain, including ankylosing spondylitis, etc.

Today there are 110 million Americans who, at certain times, need pain medications to make life bearable. How pain that is not caused by injury or infection can be produced by dehydration is simple to understand. This very simple mechanism of pain production has eluded us in medicine ever since humankind looked for a way to deal with some of the devastating pains of the human body. The drug industry spends billions of dollars researching painkillers, and even more money advertising their particular brand of pain medication. I don't believe the answer is in these medications. Dehydration can be cured by water, for free.

To understand the mechanism of pain production in the body, we first need to learn about the way the acid-alkaline balance in the body works. An acidic environment causes irritation of certain nerve endings in the body. When this irritation occurs, the brain is alerted about the chemical environmental change, which is translated and manifested as pain in the conscious mind. In other words, it is the acidity in the interior of the body that causes pain.

Normally, when blood that contains an ample amount of water circulates around the cells of the body, some of the water goes into the cells and brings out hydrogen molecules. Water washes the acidity out of the cell and makes the cell interior alkaline - an absolutely essential and normal state. For optimum health, the body should maintain an alkaline state pH - 7.4 is the desired level.

Why 7.4 and what is pH? This scale is known as pH. From 1-7 on this scale is the acid range, one being more acid than seven. From seven to 14 on the scale is the alkaline range -

seven is less alkaline than 14. On the pH scale, seven is neutral, meaning optimum. Thus, pH 7.4 of the interior of the cell denotes it's natural, slightly alkaline state. This state promotes health because it is the state that best suits the enzymes that function inside a cell; they achieve optimum efficience at this pH. Adequate flow of water in and out of the cell keeps the cell interior in its health-maintaining alkaline state.

In our bodies, the kidneys mop up excess hydrogen ions - which cause acidity - from the blood and excretes them through the urine that is formed. *The more urine that is produced, the more easily the body keeps its interior alkaline.* This is why clear urine is an indication of an efficient and clearing mechanism, and dark yellow or orange urine is an ominous sign of impending problems in the interior of the body. People who consider having to pass urine more than two or three times a day inconvenient, and do not drink water so they do not have to urinate more than they can help, are ignorant of how they are hurting their bodies.

The brain is better protected against acid buildup by the fact that it gets priority for delivery of water for all its needs. The rest of the body may not be so fortunate when dehydration establishes itself in the body and settles in one or another part for a long period of time. With persistent dehydration, however, the brain, too, becomes damaged from acidity in the cells - hence conditions such as Alzheimer's disease, multiple sclerosis, and Parkinson's disease.

From Dr. Batmanghelidj's book, "Water for Health, for Healing, for Life," pages 91-94.

EXCERPTS FROM TED'S REMEDIES

Ted from Bangkok, Thailand
earthclinic.com - 8/05/05

> *"Benjamin Franklin mentioned in his autobiography that when he had a cold, he went to the sea and drank the water. The water was full of salt, so he was cured the next day."*

I am surprised that some people are not aware of the amazing sea salt! In Thailand I use Thai sea salt. But any sea salt would do. But based on the Thai sea salt I use here, it is a very effective antibiotic!

Sea salt is the world's oldest antibiotic known to man. Somewhere along the way, history books have forgotten this great medicine that bacteria and viruses offer absolutely no resistance whatsoever. It is the simplest medicine I have ever known.

No, you don't need Himalayan sea salt, or Dead Sea salt. For me the local Thai sea salt works amazingly well. Sea salt does not raise blood pressure that much. What raises your blood pressure is usually the common salt you buy from the supermarket.

Yes, sea salt has antiviral properties. Not convinced enough? Well, some time ago ... I had a terrible urinary tract infection that lasted for weeks. After trying antiobotics from A to Z, nothing worked. ... Then I finally tested two teaspoons of sea salt and the pain subsided within minutes. Just one dose seems to have a long-term killing effect and it was completely gone without even the slightest pain within seven days.

I am writing an entire single issue on sea salt. It will take me days, but it will be enough for you to begin trying it.

[For this entire article, see www.watercure.com]

"IF WE HAD SET OUT TO DESIGN THE WORST HEALTH CARE SYSTEM THAT WE COULD IMAGINE, WE COULDN'T HAVE IMAGINED ONE AS BAD AS THE ONE WE HAVE."

By Marcia Angell, M.D.
Former *New England Journal of Medicine Editor-in-Chief*

Are we in a health care crisis?

We *certainly are* in a health care crisis.

If we had set out to design the worst system that we could imagine, we couldn't have imagined one as bad as we have.

Here's a system in which we spend over twice what the next most expensive country spends on health care - that's Switzerland.

We spent roughly $6,714 for every Americana in 2006, whether they had insurance or not.

Well, we certainly don't get our money's worth. We have roughly 43 million people with no insurance.

MAYO CLINIC TELLS HOW TO PREVENT HEART ATTACKS WITH WATER

According to Mayo Clinic experts, the risk of a winter heart attack is at least 30% higher in the first few hours after waking. "After a long night's rest, most of us are quite dehydrated, which makes blood sticky and can trigger dangerous blood clots," explains Richard M. Fleming, M.D., medical director of the Fleming Heart and Health Institute in Omaha, Nebraska. Fortunately, you can easily erase the risk by drinking an eight-ounce glass of water within 15 minutes of waking.

WHY THE WATER CURE WORKS
by Bob Butts.

Why the water cure works! It's the "Golden Rule" in action and is successful to the degree it helps you get well!

Water Cure/Golden Rule logic will solve or greatly reduce all problems!

Water Cure succeeds for the opposite reason governments and most power groups fail. It values people definitely more!

It is impossible to fail at almost anything where people are valued far more than money and power.

UPTON SINCLAIR ON SALARY

"It is difficult to get a man to understand something when his salary depends on not understanding it." *–Upton Sinclair*

> **Message from Bob Butts:** Is this why medical science and the news media ignore the free water cure?

THE QUALITY OF LIFE

Though we may have the greatest academic, political and oratory skills, we are still only assets to ourselves, humanity and our nation to the degree we are great at being kind, compassionate and ethical. They are the values that determine the quality of life everywhere. Their lack is the reason the world is in chaos today. To think otherwise is like building great cars without steering wheels and expecting them to take us where we want to go. Let us make kindness, compassion and being ethical #1, and we will improve every aspect of our lives at no cost. *–Bob Butts*

QUOTES FROM "WATER: RX FOR A HEALTHIER PAIN-FREE LIFE"

"I put the book *Your Body's Many Cries for Water)* next to the bible. I read them both."

–Dick Gregory

"One man's solution to roaring health costs *(Your Body's Many Cries for Water)*."

–Paul Harvey

"The water principle...turns much of current medical practice on its head. Does it work? You only have to turn on the water to find out."

–*The European*, London

"(Dr. Batmanghelidj) has successfully treated allergies, angina, asthma, arthritis, headaches, hypertension, ulcers and more with the simplest of solutions–water."

–*Nexus Magazine*, Australia

"Dr. Batmanghelidj gives examples of patients who have followed his advice using ordinary tap water with positive results in reducing blood pressure, allergy relief and weight loss. He even goes so far as to link the lack of water with depression.."

–*The Irish Times*

"I think this reading this book should be made compulsory to all the Elementary, Middle and High Schools."

–Hizen Shah, M.D., San Jacinto Medical Center, CA

"The Greatest Health Discovery in the World."

–Sam Biser, The University of Natural Healing

"Batmanghelidj's book *(Your Body's Many Cries for Water)* hits the nail on the head period."

–Arthur Moll, D.C.

"The content of your book *(Your Body's Many Cries for Water)* is a huge gulp of fresh air, and holds much hope for the human race!"

–Judge John H. Morgan, California

"It does seem logical to adhere to the natural and the simple in medicine, as fostered in the book, *Your Body's Many Cries for Water.*

—Monsignor Philip A. Gray, Scranton, PA

"When I make a conscious effort to drink water, I never get that starving feeling. When I sit down to eat, I don't eat that much."

—Julie Moran, *ET*

"I drink water to lose weight. (From article in *Woman's World)*

—Finola Hughes, *All My Children*

DRINKING WATER COULD CURB OBESITY

Excerpts from an article in the archives of Pediatric and Adolescent Medicine
by Sherry Baker, Health Science Editor
Based on a
Study by the Center for Disease Control and the Robert Wood Johnson Foundation

It's not just American adults who are faced with an epidemic of obesity. Children and adolescents are becoming overweight at an alarming rate. In fact, Center for Disease Control (CDC) statistics show the prevalence of obesity among children between the ages of 6 and 11 has more than doubled in the past 20 years.

That's the conclusion of the researchers from *Columbia University Mailman School of Public Health* and the *Harvard*

School of Public Health, who authored the study. They analyzed what children and teens reported they ate and drank over two different days, using nationally representative data from the 2003-2004 *National Health and Nutrition Examination Survey.* They then estimated what substituting water for (sugar-sweetened drinks) would mean to the total energy intake of youngsters between the ages of 2 to 19. The result? Drinking water instead of sugary drinks could eliminate an average of 235 excess calories per day among children and adolescents.

"This study shows the substantial impact that replacing sugar-sweetened beverages with water could have," stated C. Tracy Orleans, Senior Scientist and distinguished fellow at the Robert Wood Johnson Foundation, which co-funded the study along with the CDC.

See Chapter Ten: Obesity

SCHOOL WATER FOUNTAINS TO PREVENT OBESITY

New York Times

"Could this be the answer to childhood obesity?" —George Ruhe for the New York Times

Adding school water fountains, distributing water bottles in classrooms and teaching kids abut the health benefits of water can lower a child's risk for becoming overweight, a new study shows.

The findings published in *Pediatrics*, are based on a unique intervention in 12 German grade schools. In the study, about 2,000 second and third graders were weighed and quizzed about their beverage consumption. In some of the schools, water fountains were added and children were given personal water bottles they could fill at the beginning of the school day. Teachers were also given lesson plans that include health messages about the benefits of water consumption.

At the beginning of the study, there were no statistical differences in the prevalence of overweight kids in the different groups. By the end of the school year, however, children in the schools where water drinking was encouraged were 30 percent less likely to be overweight.

See Chapter Ten: Obesity

EPILOGUE

☞ By Dr. Batmanghelidj and Bob Butts

EPILOGUE

The wisdom of the late Dr. B. in his own words, is a fitting epilogue for this book along with a final word from Bob Butts, who has "taken the reins" of the Water Cure.

"*The common cause of the illnesses listed in this book is chronic dehydration.* That is why when people do the Water Cure and are no longer dehydrated, many so-called 'incurable' problems go away.

"Dehydration, thanks to consuming diuretic caffeinated, alcoholic, or soda drinks, devastates our immune systems and turns our pH acidic. This compromises our immune systems to the degree our bodies are dehydrated and acidic. It is impossible for any drug or procedure, other than a saline IV, to entirely effect any problem caused by dehydration. That is why I say 'You are not sick, you are thirsty.'

"If the Water Cure were followed according to my book, '*Your body's many Cries for Water*,' we could save hundreds of thousands of Americans yearly from slow, painful, premature deaths while cutting health costs down to a fraction of what they are today. The savings would be more than enough to save the physical and financial health of our nation and millions of jobs. The money saved on health care is far more than enough to fund the reopening of our manufacturing, provided we change the way we live... that is, to recognize that being ethical must be the foundation of our new birth."

F. Batmanghelidj, M.D.

The only expense relative to the Water Cure is for your food and a few supplements. You will also need to get Dr. Batmanghelidj's books or, in many areas, you can borrow them.

The #1 desire of humanity - "Avoid pain and gain pleasure." Healing should never cause pain or result in uncomfortable side effects.

I think that anyone who got well after using the Water Cure solution should get a 200% refund for all of the money wasted that failed them. There would be a lot more incentive to do what is right instead of what is profitable.

–Bob Butts

MEET AUTHOR HARRIET CLYDE KIPPS, EDITOR-IN-CHIEF OF *"TRIUMPH OVER PAIN"*

With President Ronald Reagan

With First Lady Barbara Bush

Harriet Clyde Kipps is a lifelong volunteer. She was honored in the Oval Office for her humanitarian work, commended before Congress, and worked with John Glenn, Barbara Bush, Colin Powell, Congresswoman Cardiss Collins, Dr. Bill Cosby, Eugene Lang (I Have a Dream Foundation), and Miss America (Dr. Debby Turner), among others, on volunteer issues.

She has written 30 books on volunteerism, including "Volunteer America" and "Volunteerism," each of which includes program descriptions in 36 areas of service to the community. She has received the Jefferson Award three times. She formed nationwide "Super Volunteers Clubs" for children to learn about helping their communities *(which numbered 2,400 members in five states the first year)*, and a children's book series, *"The*

Super Volunteers Club Mysteries," to give them the adventure they seek with a sub-theme on volunteering that children can safely do.

She has used proceeds from her books for local projects, including the rehabilitation of a playground in a small town, and nationwide projects, such as providing her children's books to "Tuesday's Children" for distribution to the children of 9/11.

She is a true humanitarian and has embraced the work of the late F. Batmanghelidj, M.D., discoverer of the miracle Water Cure, and Bob Butts, who has taken the reins of the Water Cure so that you can receive this book, and also learn from his work about the Water Cure's healing and life-saving powers. kippsharriet@yahoo.com

With Astronaut/Senator John Glenn

With Statesman/General Colin Powell

MY OWN WATER CURE JOURNAL

Message from Bob Butts:

This journal is for you to record notes, thoughts, questions for the Water Cure Team (see page iii), names, addresses and/or phones of Water Cure consultants, and/or a record of your progress if you decide to try the "Water Cure."

_____

_____

_____

_____

_____

_____

_____

_____

_____

_____

_____

MY OWN WATER CURE JOURNAL

_____

_____

_____

_____

_____

_____

_____

_____

_____

_____

_____

_____

_____

_____

_____

_____

MY OWN WATER CURE JOURNAL

_____

_____

_____

_____

_____

_____

_____

_____

_____

_____

_____

_____

_____

_____

_____

_____

_____

MY OWN WATER CURE JOURNAL

53221 eplit
1610 ot octes

Made in the USA
Charleston, SC
17 April 2012